INSPIRE / PLAN / DISCOVER / FXPERIENCE

WASHINGTON, DC

WASHINGTON, DC

CONTENTS

DISCOVER 6

EXPERIENCE 48

NEED TO KNOW 190

Left: The Rotunda at the United States Capitol
Previous page: The Washington Monument seen from the Lincoln Memorial
Front cover: Reflections in the Lincoln Memorial pool

DISCOVER

Bird's-eye view of the Lincoln Memorial

WELCOME TO
WASHINGTON, DC

Museums filled with wonders. Galleries bursting with masterworks. Lush, verdant parks and gardens. And everywhere famous views that every visitor knows by heart. This is a city in renaissance, a grand dream of marble and art, of substance and spectacle. Wherever you turn, there are iconic sights - the White House, the Lincoln Memorial, the US Capitol, and much more. Whatever your dream trip to Washington, DC entails, this DK Eyewitness travel guide is the perfect companion.

1 The Potomac in Mather Gorge, Great Falls.

2 Statue of Franklin D. Roosevelt's terrier at his memorial.

3 Aircraft at the National Air and Space Museum.

4 The Jefferson Memorial at the Tidal Basin.

Washington, DC is bursting with exciting neighborhoods that have been rebuilt and reborn. In recent years the city has revitalized its waterfront, building gardens and bike paths along the Potomac River, and creating fabulous waterfront developments like National Harbor and District Wharf.

The heart of the city is the National Mall, ringed with grand museums and monuments. Science comes to life among the dinosaurs of the National Museum of Natural History, while spacecraft inspires the future at the National Air and Space Museum. The Northwest district is home to the magnificent Phillips Collection and the historic Howard University. Georgetown offers chic shopping and elegant rowhouses that were once inhabited by famous personalities such as the Kennedys. Capitol Hill and Penn Quarter offer fine dining and unique attractions such as the National Archives and the US Botanic Garden. U Street, an epicenter of African American culture, has an unparalleled music and nightlife scene, while vibrant Adams Morgan has a thriving international and LGBTQ+ community.

Washington, DC is a small gem, so packed with attractions that it can be hard to know where to start. We've broken the city down into easily navigable chapters, with detailed itineraries, expert local knowledge, and colorful, comprehensive maps to help you plan the perfect visit. Whether you're staying for a weekend or longer, this DK Eyewitness guide will ensure that you see the very best America's capital has to offer. Enjoy the book, and enjoy Washington, DC.

REASONS TO LOVE
WASHINGTON, DC

It may be a compact city but Washington, DC delights at every turn. Any list of its treasures must include its famed museums, magnificent memorials, green spaces, and secret sanctuaries. Here are a few of our favorites.

1 THE NATIONAL MALL

Often called "America's front yard," the National Mall *(p62)* is an amazing collection of museums, gardens, and beautiful memorials that are the centerpiece of America's capital.

AMAZING ARCHITECTURE *2*

The city's architects want you to know that this is an important city, and they do it with architectural eye candy, from the Neo-Classical Supreme Court *(p56)* to the Beaux Arts Union Station *(p59)*.

3 TIDAL BASIN

An unexpected treat on the west end of the National Mall is this scenic pool *(p84)*, edged by a walking path that offers post-card views and shaded places to sit beneath the cherry trees.

NATIONAL GALLERY OF ART 4

One of the world's greatest collections, the gallery *(p66)* has works ranging from antiquities to pop art, including *Multiverse*, this striking light sculpture by Leo Villareal.

UNITED STATES CAPITOL 5

This iconic building, which has been featured in many movies such as *Mr. Smith Goes to Washington* (1939) and *Independence Day* (1996), is a symbol of the nation's strength.

LINCOLN MEMORIAL 6

As well as a memorial to the sixteenth US president, this statue *(p84)* is a touchstone for the Civil Rights movement and a symbol of social justice. The upper steps offer the best view of the National Mall anywhere.

CHERRY BLOSSOMS 7

Few things can compare to walking beneath cherry trees with clouds of delicate blossoms. Originally a gift from Japan, thousands of cherry trees now stand in the National Mall area *(p62)*. They bloom from late March to early April.

THE RIVERFRONT 8

The Potomac *(p26)* has become a symbol of the city's renaissance. Cycling and walking paths and lush parks line the river's edge, and its waters teem with boaters.

9 DISTRICT WHARF

This multibillion-dollar development *(p136)* offers riverfront dining, marinas, and shopping and concerts by the water. The Wharf jitney is the cheapest cruise in DC (it's free!).

10 GEORGETOWN

Cobblestoned Georgetown *(p118)* is DC's most historic district. Relax on a sunny afternoon at the waterfront park, or people-watch at Dean & DeLuca.

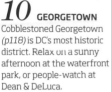

A SEAT IN THE GALLERIES 11

One of the great things about Washington, DC is that you can witness the government in action. Watch Supreme Court *(p56)* arguments or bills being passed in the Capitol *(p54)*.

MARVELOUS MUSEUMS 12

Washington's many museums are packed with spectacular exhibits, such as *Musical Crossroads* at the National Museum of African American History and Culture *(p78)*.

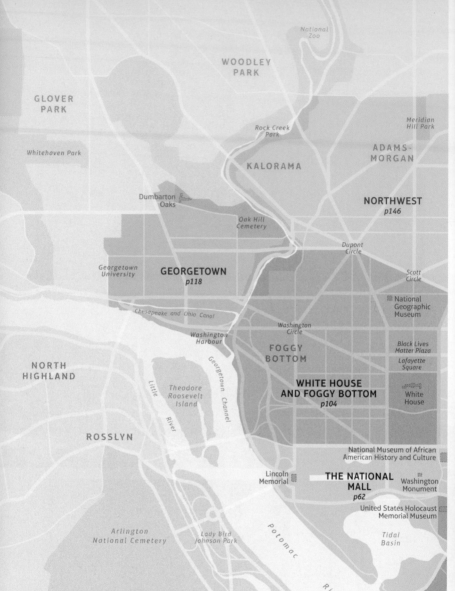

National Zoo

WOODLEY
PARK

GLOVER
PARK

Meridian
Hill Park

Whitehaven Park

Rock Creek
Park

ADAMS-
MORGAN

KALORAMA

NORTHWEST
p146

Dumbarton
Oaks

Oak Hill
Cemetery

Dupont
Circle

Georgetown
University

GEORGETOWN
p118

Scott
Circle

National
Geographic
Museum

Chesapeake and Ohio Canal

Washington
Circle

Washington
Harbour

Black Lives
Matter Plaza

FOGGY
BOTTOM

Lafayette
Square

NORTH
HIGHLAND

Theodore
Roosevelt
Island

Georgetown Channel

WHITE HOUSE
AND FOGGY BOTTOM
p104

White
House

Little River

ROSSLYN

National Museum of African
American History and Culture

Lincoln
Memorial

THE NATIONAL
MALL
p62

Washington
Monument

United States Holocaust
Memorial Museum

Arlington
National Cemetery

Lady Bird
Johnson Park

Potomac

River

Tidal
Basin

EXPLORE
WASHINGTON, DC

This guide divides Washington, DC into seven color-coded
sightseeing areas, as shown on the map above. Find out
more about each area on the following pages. For sights
beyond the city center see p158, and for day trips out of
Washington, DC see p174.

COLUMBIA
HEIGHTS

CARDOZO-
SHAW

Howard
University

African American
Civil War Museum

Logan
Circle

Mt Vernon
Square

SAAM
and NPG

PENN
QUARTER
p88

National
Archives

National Museum
of Natural History

National Gallery
of Art

National Air and
Space Museum

Museum of
the Bible

International
Spy Museum

SOUTH OF
THE NATIONAL MALL
p132

District
Wharf

WATERFRONT

East
Potomac
Park

Washington Channel

Nationals
Park

Navy Yard
Park

Navy
Museum

Gallaudet
University

Columbus
Circle

CAPITOL HILL
p50

Stanton
Square

US
Capitol

Seward
Square

Lincoln
Park

ANACOSTIA

Anacostia River

NORTH AMERICA

CANADA

• Seattle

USA

• San Francisco

• Los Angeles

Chicago •

WASHINGTON, DC •

Memphis •

• Atlanta

Houston •

Gulf of
Mexico

MEXICO

Pacific
Ocean

• Boston

• New York

Atlantic
Ocean

• Miami

0 kilometers   1

0 miles   0.5

N
↑

GETTING TO KNOW
WASHINGTON, DC

America's capital is the seat of government. It is also a massively popular destination, with tens of millions of visitors each year. For those ready to explore beyond museums and monuments, there is a colorful collection of distinctive neighborhoods, each with its own personality and pulse.

PAGE 50

CAPITOL HILL

The Capitol may be the most iconic image of American democracy in the world. A tour of the building, with its ornate architecture, remarkable artworks, and world-shaping history, is a great place to start. An easy walk away lie the exquisite Union Station, the historic shops of Eastern Market, and block after block of elegant row houses.

Best for
Watching the governing of the United States

Home to
United States Capitol

Experience
A tour of the grand Capitol building and lunch at Eastern Market

PAGE 62

THE NATIONAL MALL

The place everyone wants to see, but no one can see it all – there are 11 museums alone here. The National Mall is a glorious 2-mile- (3.5-km-) long swath of emerald lawn, dotted by park-like spaces and gardens. It is bordered on the eastern half by some of the world's most famous museums and on the western half by grand memorials to the nation's leaders and history.

Best for
Monuments and museums

Home to
National Air and Space Museum, National Museum of African American History and Culture

Experience
The view across the National Mall from the Lincoln Memorial

PAGE 88

PENN QUARTER

Penn Quarter is business-casual. Home to famous nonprofits, lobbyist groups, and think tanks, this neighborhood also offers fine restaurants, lesser-known memorials, and a handful of truly wonderful, if quirky, museums. The area is also home to several food and wine festivals and a popular weekly farmers market outside the Smithsonian American Art Museum (SAAM).

Best for
Fascinating, lesser-known museums

Home to
SAAM and National Portrait Gallery

Experience
The vast collection of American art at the Smithsonian American Art Museum (SAAM)

PAGE 104

WHITE HOUSE AND FOGGY BOTTOM

The grand centerpiece of this area is the Executive Mansion, also known as the White House. If you do not manage to get tickets for a tour, you can still enjoy the iconic views of the mansion from the north and south sides. Lafayette Square offers great people-watching and is surrounded by historic homes and buildings. Also in this area are the renowned Renwick Gallery and the Kennedy Center.

Best for
Strolling through Lafayette Park, enjoying the famous views of the White House and watching the ever-present protesters, bustling news crews, and throngs of tourists from around the world

Home to
The White House

Experience
Perusing the artifacts and multimedia displays in the White House Visitor Center

→

PAGE 118

GEORGETOWN

Elegant and cool, Georgetown is a hub of education, history, culture, and outdoor activities all rolled into one. Its historic row houses have seen a who's who of residents, from Thomas Jefferson to the Kennedys. Nature beckons in the stunning gardens of Dumbarton Oaks and along the lovely Chesapeake and Ohio Canal. This is also DC's most established shopping and dining area.

Best for
Shopping, dining, enjoying the outdoors

Home to
Chesapeake and Ohio Canal, Dumbarton Oaks

Experience
A paddle on the Potomac (rent a kayak at Thompson Boat Center), and shopping at the one-of-a-kind Sunday Georgetown Flea Market

PAGE 132

SOUTH OF THE NATIONAL MALL

District Wharf (or locally just "the Wharf") is a glittering mini-city. This is where the river lives. Four piers, two marinas, and two parks offer boat tours, live riverfront music, a thriving seafood market, water taxis, and lots of places to watch the river roll by.

Best for
Waterfront dining and strolling

Home to
United States Holocaust Memorial Museum

Experience
Fresh steamed seafood at Captain White's, and a water taxi ride – a fun, cheap cruise

PAGE 146

NORTHWEST

The western part of Northwest is full of 100-year-old mansions built by the wealthy; to the east, the culturally influential African American neighborhoods of U Street and Shaw were once known as the "Black Broadway." Today, this is one of the city's most vibrant areas.

Best for
Great architecture, lively music and entertainment

Home to
Embassy Row

Experience
Renoir's Afternoon of the Boating Party at the Phillips Collection, followed by dinner and a show at the Howard Theater

BEYOND THE CENTER

Just outside the popular tourist areas are a number of remarkable attractions waiting to be explored. There is George Washington's beloved home, Mount Vernon; the National Arlington Cemetery, the resting place of American soldiers; and a Gothic cathedral whose grotesques include Darth Vader. There are some wonderful parks and gardens too, such as the lush National Arboretum, the aquatic Kenilworth, and the wooded Theodore Roosevelt Island.

Best for
History, parks, and cathedrals

Home to
Mount Vernon, National Arlington Cemetery

Experience
Meeting artists at Old Town Alexandria's Torpedo Factory, and watching whiskey being made at Mount Vernon's distillery

DAYS OUT FROM WASHINGTON, DC

There are a wealth of unique attractions within one to three hours' drive of the city. Marvel at the Blue Ridge Mountains on a road trip along Skyline Drive in Shenandoah National Park. The Udvar-Hazy Center has all the fabulous air- and spacecraft that the Smithsonian could not fit in their museum on the National Mall. Annapolis was briefly the nation's capital, and today is a sailing town with a lot of history and plenty of fine dining. Farther out, the magnificent Colonial Williamsburg site re-creates an 18th-century town with over 100 restored buildings and costumed interpreters.

Best for
Charming historic towns such as Frederick, Middleburg, and Charlottesville

Home to
Colonial Williamsburg, Udvar-Hazy Center, Skyline Drive

Experience
The flight simulators at the Udvar-Hazy Center that let you pilot a fighter jet or blast off into space, and a chat with the reenactors at Colonial Williamsburg

←

1 Planes at the National Air and Space Museum.

2 Calder's *Cheval Rouge* (1974), Sculpture Garden.

3 Van Gogh's *Self Portrait* (1889), National Gallery of Art.

4 Blues Alley, Georgetown.

With its monuments and museums, ravishing restaurants, and sumptuous shopping, Washington, DC is a feast for travelers. These itineraries are intended to be your friend in the city, helping you see the best that America's capital has to offer.

2 DAYS

Day 1

Morning Start your day rocketing into space on an Apollo mission or flying with the Wright Brothers on simulators at the National Air and Space Museum (p70). Arrive early and be sure to see the *Wright Flyer*, the *Spirit of St. Louis*, and the *Lunar Module*. Afterward, walk across the National Mall to the Sculpture Garden at the National Gallery of Art (p66) to admire works by Chagall and Calder. Enjoy lunch on the patio of the Pavilion Café.

Afternoon Stroll around the world and through time at the National Gallery of Art. Choose from Byzantine, Renaissance, and Impressionist collections, or visit the East Wing for modern art. Next walk east along the National Mall, then north around the White House (p108). Enjoy the iconic views and linger for a while in Lafayette Square or see the murals on Black Lives Matter Plaza (p112). Then it's back to the National Mall and the Lincoln Memorial (p84) to stand at the feet of the statue and read the Gettysburg Address engraved on the wall.

Evening Finish your evening at the legendary Blues Alley (p125) in Georgetown. One of the oldest and most famous jazz venues in the country, it has hosted a plethora of musical greats such as Ella Fitzgerald, Sarah Vaughan, and Dizzy Gillespie.

Day 2

Morning A stroll through the beautiful, dew-laden Enid A. Haupt Garden is a great way to start the morning before you head across the National Mall to the National Museum of Natural History (p74). There is a lot to see here, including the towering dinosaur skeletons, the Hope Diamond (and hundreds of other dazzling gems), and the carefully reconstructed faces of our early ancestors in the Hall of Human Origins.

Afternoon Pause for lunch at the United States Capitol Cafe, whose gleaming serving stations provide far more delicious fare than its name suggests. If you haven't prebooked your Capitol (p54) tour online, go to the information booth, where there may still be timed-entry tickets available. After your tour, cool down by strolling through the stunning conservatory and grounds of the US Botanic Garden (p58).

Evening Come evening, make for local favorite Zaytina (p99), run by award-winning chef and humanitarian José Andrés, for Mediterranean-style mezze. Round off the evening with a cocktail or two at one of Penn Quarter's lively bars. Our pick is the cosy Denson Liquor Bar (www.densondc.com).

←

1 The mansion and gardens at Mount Vernon.

2 Washington National Cathedral.

3 Old Town Alexandria.

4 Walkway around Tidal Basin.

4 DAYS

Day 1

Morning An enlightening morning awaits at the National Museum of African American History and Culture (p78). The exhibits begin with slavery, followed by aspects of African American culture. Lunch north of the White House on fresh fare at Founding Farmers (www.wearefoundingfarmers.com).

Afternoon Stroll around the White House perimeter (p108), taking in the famous views, then explore three centuries of American culture at the Smithsonian American Art Museum (p92). Be sure to see the "Experience America" exhibit for a look at art across the 1930s.

Evening Dine at Captain White's Seafood (www.captainwhitesseafood.com) on the riverfront. After dinner, walk around the National Mall's monuments, which are beautifully lit after dark.

Day 2

Morning What better way to start your morning than with a stroll around the Tidal Basin, stopping to explore the Jefferson Memorial (p85) and Franklin D. Roosevelt Memorial (p85). After, head to the National Museum of American History (p76) and try the burgers and barbeque at its America's Table restaurant.

Afternoon Time to explore American history: stop to gaze at the (yes, the) Star-Spangled Banner. Then walk across the National Mall to enjoy the Asian and American art at the Freer Gallery of Art (p82).

Evening For dinner, head to Mi Vida (p137), a high-end Mexican restaurant with views of the Washington Channel.

Day 3

Morning Start your day meandering through the sunlit gardens of Mount Vernon (p162), George Washington's beloved estate. Enjoy an early lunch at the busy onsite bistro, Mount Vernon Inn, before heading 4 miles (6.5 km) down the road to see the gristmill and distillery, Washington's most successful businesses.

Afternoon Explore charming Old Town Alexandria (p166). Start at the Torpedo Factory Art Center, a World War II munitions factory that now houses artists' studios. A stroll around the historic core and some shopping, with a stop for ice cream, rounds off your afternoon.

Evening When you are ready for dinner, head to the elegant, French-inspired Le Refuge for a delicious evening meal (www.lerefugealexandria.com).

Day 4

Morning Start at the Gothic Washington National Cathedral (p164) with a bit of gargoyle-spotting. Then, head to the Phillips Collection (p150) to peruse its line-up of stunning modern art. Nearby, Zorba's Café (www.zorbascafedc.com) on Dupont Circle is the go-to for a tasty Greek lunch.

Afternoon Admire exceptional American crafts at the Renwick Gallery (p113). Then it's on to the National Archives (p96) to view the original Declaration of Independence.

Evening Stroll to the beautiful Union Station (p59), and kick back at East Street Café (www.eaststreetcafe.com), with its stellar views of the station's soaring, gilded ceilings, for a relaxing end-of-vacation evening.

Dine with DC's Movers and Shakers

The city is famed for its old-school restaurants where presidents, politicians, and power brokers meet to make deals, or just relax. Follow in the footsteps of former US presidents by dining on fresh oysters at Old Ebbitt Grill (*www.ebbitt.com*), or have a steak at Martin's Tavern (*p125*), a favorite of President Harry S. Truman in the 1940s.

←

The oyster bar at Old Ebbit Grill, Washington, DC's oldest restaurant

WASHINGTON, DC FOR
FOODIES

Foodies are in for a treat in Washington, DC. Just about every type of cuisine is available here – Eritrean to Italian, Korean to Colombian – with prices ranging from $5.99 for a simple bowl of chili to exquisite gourmet fare at some of the world's most exclusive farm-to-table restaurants.

BLUE CRABS FROM THE BAY

Along with Baltimore and all the cities of the Chesapeake watershed, Washington, DC enjoys the annual Chesapeake Bay crab season. Better known as blue crabs, these salty, sweet delicacies are traditionally steamed fresh and served with old bay seasoning (a blend of herbs and spices made in Baltimore). The blue crab season starts from April and lasts all the way through to December. It's best to purchase the crabs live or have them cooked at Captain White Seafood City (*www.captainwhite-seafood.com*).

DC Markets and Food Courts

With multiple food stalls serving everything from Vietnamese pho to pumpkin cupcakes in one place, gourmet food halls and markets are popular in DC. Eastern Market (*p57*) has stalls of farm-fresh produce, while Union Market (*www.unionmarketdc.com*), chock-full of snack vendors, offers Korean tacos, shrimp and grits, pesto-and-egg sandwiches, and much more.

An airstream camper converted into a food stall in Union Market ↑

Washington, DC Food Icons

Hot dogs smothered in chili sauce, gooey grilled cheese sandwiches, and finger-licking maple bacon doughnuts are just some of the iconic dishes that are associated with DC. The popular Chili Half Smoke (hot dog in chili sauce) at Ben's Chili Bowl *(p151)*, the cheese sandwiches with a cult-like following at Stoney's *(www.stoneys-dc.com)*, the hearty G Man Subs (ham-and-cheese sandwiches) at Mangialardo's *(www.mangialardos.com)*, and fluffy maple bacon doughnuts at Astro *(www. astrodoughnuts.com)* are all must-tries.

INSIDER TIP
Food Tours

Food walking tours are a great way to see the city and try delicious cuisines. Top tours include DC Metro Food Tours *(www.dcmetro-foodtours.co)* and Mangia DC Food Tours *(mangiadc.com)*.

↑ Ben's Chili Bowl at U Street, an iconic and historic DC eatery

Southern Soul Food and BBQ

Washington, DC is the gateway to the American South and is home to numerous restaurants dedicated to classic soul food and Southern-style BBQ. Sweet potato pie, slab pork ribs, wings, and other African American dishes can be found at Henry's Soul Café *(p151)*. DC's best BBQ joints are DCity Smokehouse *(www.dcitysmokhouse.com)*, known for smoked wings and mac and cheese, and Texas-style meat specialist Hill Country Barbecue Market *(p99)*.

←
Succulent pork ribs served with baked beans at DCity Smokehouse

Ethiopian and Eritrean Eats

Many Ethiopian and Eritrean refugees settled in DC in the 1970s and 1980s, and as a result the city is a hotspot for East African cuisine. Savor injera flatbread and wat stews at Ethiopian restaurants Zenebech *(www.zenebech dc.com)* and Chercher *(www. chercherrestaurant.com)*, or try Eritrean kicha silsi (sourdough bread in a spicy sauce) at Keren Café *(www.order-kerencafeandrestaurant.com)*.

→
Diners enjoying Ethiopian cuisine at Zenebech

Parks and Paths

From Mount Vernon *(p162)* to Great Falls *(p184)*, the Potomac River is lined with miles of parks and well-groomed trails and paths. The Chesapeake and Ohio Canal *(p122)* towpath follows the river from Georgetown *(p118)* to Great Falls and beyond. On the west bank, the 18-mile (29-km) Mount Vernon Trail passes through Alexandria *(p166)* into Arlington, while on the east side, East Potomac Park *(p145)* is popular with families as well as walkers and cyclists. In the middle of the river, Theodore Roosevelt Island *(p170)* offers miles of hiking trails through the forest.

→

Great Falls, a popular hiking area with great views of the river in Mather Gorge

WASHINGTON, DC FOR
THE POTOMAC

Washington, DC has rediscovered its waterfront on a grand scale. Both historic towns such as Georgetown and Alexandria and modern, reinvigorated communities like District Wharf and National Harbor offer a cornucopia of restaurants, shops, parks, and entertainment along the Potomac River.

POTOMAC HISTORY

George Washington envisioned a capital that was both a commercial and political center, and believed its ideal location would be on the river between the port towns of Georgetown and Alexandria. The former was the hub of local commerce through the Civil War, while Alexandria supported trade with England. After the Civil War, and through World War II, the Potomac was lined with gambling barges and floating brothels in what was then an unregulated and tax-free zone. Today, the scenic river is primarily used for recreation.

On the River

A great way to see DC is to rent a kayak, canoe, or scull and enjoy rowing *(p128)* on the river. Cruises are available from Georgetown, Mount Vernon, District Wharf *(p136)*, National Harbor *(p173)*, and Old Town Alexandria, or you can enjoy a less expensive ride on a water taxi *(p142)* to all these places as well as Washington Harbour *(p124)* and the National Mall *(p62)*.

→

Washington Harbour, a popular place from which to get out on the water

TOP 5 POTOMAC RIVER VIEWS

Iwo Jima Memorial
Spectacular views of the city *(p170)*.

Capital Wheel
Stunning river vistas atop this giant Ferris wheel *(p173)*.

Francis Scott Key Memorial Bridge
Lovely mid-river views from one of the city's prettiest bridges *(p127)*.

Mount Vernon
Panoramic views from Washington's grand estate *(p162)*.

Great Falls
Views of wild cascades from the C&O Canal visitor center *(p184)*.

← The wooded Theodore Roosevelt Island, popular with bird-watchers and hikers

Fun on the Waterfront

National Harbor's inviting waterfront has a huge Ferris wheel and hosts festivals and a summer concert series. Street performers, festivals, and parks with picturesque city views are showcased along the river in Old Town Alexandria, while District Wharf boasts a wealth of riverside shops, restaurants, and entertainment alongside the legendary Maine Avenue Fish Market.

↑ The 180-ft-(55-m-) high Capital Wheel at National Harbor

Houses of History

DC has several museums that focus on the African American experience. One of the most impressive and informative of these is the National Museum of African American History and Culture *(p78)*. The home of Frederick Douglass is now a National Historic Site *(p172)*, while the Mary McLeod Bethune Council House National Historic Site *(p153)* preserves the legacy of the legendary educator and activist.

→

The Serenity Room at the National Museum of African American History and Culture

WE ARE DETERMINED ... TO WO
UNTIL JUSTICE RUNS DOWN LI
RIGHTEOUSNESS LIKE A MIGH

MARTIN LUTHER KING JR

Did You Know?

By 1804, all Northern states had voted to abolish slavery; in 1850, DC ended auctions of enslaved people.

WASHINGTON, DC FOR
BLACK HISTORY

Washington, DC holds a unique place in African American history. After Lincoln's Emancipation Proclamation in 1863, the city became a sanctuary for free Black people and enslaved people who had managed to escape. It was a hub of political action and protest throughout the Civil Rights era. Washington, DC has been home to renowned African Americans, including abolitionist and statesman Frederick Douglass, legendary jazzman Duke Ellington, and Barack Obama, who became the country's first African American president in 2009.

Memorials and Monuments

Several DC monuments have played a big role in African American history. The Lincoln Memorial *(p84)* was the backdrop for the iconic 1963 "I Have a Dream" speech by Dr. Martin Luther King, Jr., who is honored with a granite memorial *(p84)*. The African American Civil War Memorial *(p153)* remembers the African American soldiers who fought in the war. A section of 16th Street was officially renamed Black Lives Matter Plaza *(p112)* in 2020.

←

Martin Luther King, Jr. Memorial, Tidal Basin

MARIAN ANDERSON SINGS AT THE LINCOLN MEMORIAL

In 1939 famed classical singer Marian Anderson performed at the Lincoln Memorial for an integrated crowd. It was an important milestone after the Daughters of the American Revolution had refused to allow the African American singer to perform for an integrated audience in Constitution Hall under its "white performers-only" policy.

→

Mary McLeod Bethune, renowned educator and civil and women's rights activist

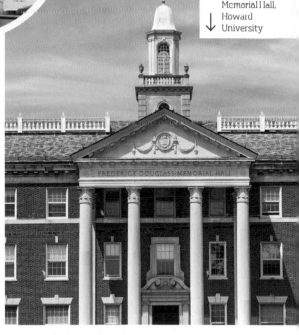

Frederick Douglass Memorial Hall, Howard University ↓

TOP 4 LESSER-KNOWN SITES

A. Philip Randolph Monument
A statue in Union Station *(p59)* of the civil rights activist.

Malcolm X Park
The unofficial name given to Meridian Hill Park in the 1960s *(p150)*.

Emancipation Monument
⦿ Q3 ⬡ Lincoln Park Dr NE
Statue of Lincoln and an enslaved person breaking free.

Sojourner Truth
A bust of the activist and abolitionist is located in the US Capitol Visitor Center *(p54)*.

Cultural Touchstones

The Lincoln Theatre *(p155)*, a mainstay of the "Black Broadway" in the 1930s and 40s, today presents an array of multicultural entertainment. Howard University *(p152)*, one of the country's first institutes of higher learning for Black people, is now a top choice for African Americans enrolled in prestigious science, technology, engineering, and math (STEM) programs.

Ponds in the Constitution
Gardens reflecting the ↑
Washington Monument

WASHINGTON, DC FOR

GARDENS AND GREEN SPACES

Washington, DC's beautiful parks and gardens are among its unsung delights.
You are never far from a place with cool green shade, fountains, flowers, and
inviting benches. There are traditional gardens bursting with color, lovely
parks with paths and ponds, special-purpose green spaces like the National
Arboretum, and outdoor destinations such as the Great Falls Park nearby.

Fabulous Flowers

Flowers, flowers everywhere.
The 1920s gardens of Dumbarton
Oaks *(p125)* are elegant and
lovely, with an air of Victorian
mystery. Mount Vernon *(p162)*
has re-created the gardens that
George Washington would have
enjoyed, and the entire Capitol
Grounds are a large, park-like
space with the US Botanic Garden
(p58) at its center. But perhaps
the ultimate Washington, DC
garden experience is an early
springtime walk along the edge of
the Tidal Basin *(p84)*, under the
arched, blooming branches of the
exquisite cherry trees.

→

Flowering plants and
greenhouses at the
US Botanic Garden

Shaded Green Spaces

A wealth of green spaces offers moments of quietude and beauty. On the National Mall *(p62)*, a tranquil pond, its edges traced by tree-shaded paths, is the centerpiece of Constitution Gardens. Along the Potomac, Georgetown Waterfront Park *(p129)* is a bustling family-friendly space, while away from the river to the north, Rock Creek Park *(p171)* boasts a stream-side path that is a favorite with walkers, joggers, and cyclists.

← Kids enjoying a cooling water feature at the Georgetown Waterfront Park

TOP 4 LITTLE-KNOWN GARDENS

Bishop's Garden
A lovely walled garden outside the National Cathedral *(p164)*.

Lady Bird Johnson Park
📍 C9
Flower-filled park stretching along the banks of the Potomac.

Enid A. Haupt Garden
Blossom-laden park set behind the Smithsonian Castle *(p80)*.

Hirshhorn Sculpture Garden
Tranquil walled garden opposite the Hirshhorn Museum *(p81)* with magnificent sculptures.

🔍 HIDDEN GEM Pershing Park

Surrounded by busy streets, Pershing Park is a watery sanctuary near the White House. It is home to the National World War I Memorial.

Pagoda tucked away in the lush foliage of the National Arboretum ↑

Parks with Purpose

Washington, DC has a number of park-like spaces that have a purpose beyond beauty. Chief among them is the National Arboretum *(p172)*, whose 446 acres (180 ha), while a research space for botanists, are simply a magnificent green space filled with trees and flower-lined paths for visitors. The National Zoo *(p170)* is a glorious park and a favorite with kids, but it is also a respected conservation center and home to endangered species such as scimitar-horned oryx and red pandas.

All American

Art that expresses the American experience is huge in Washington, DC. The best places to engage with contemporary art are the Renwick Gallery *(p113)* and the Smithsonian American Art Museum *(p92)*. The latter holds an extraordinary piece by Nam June Paik called *Electronic Superhighway*, a 50-channel video installation. The National Portrait Gallery *(p92)* holds paintings and images of Americans who have played an influential role in the country's history.

Did You Know?

In the 1960s, the Washington Color School, an abstract art movement, put DC on the art world map.

WASHINGTON, DC FOR
ART LOVERS

Washington, DC is one of the nation's stellar art and culture destinations, its museums and galleries displaying some of the most dazzling collections in the country. Alongside this, the performing arts scene offers world-class recitals and shows as well as cutting-edge theater in small venues.

Dazzling Masterpieces

The acclaimed National Gallery of Art *(p66)* holds European and American masterpieces in a variety of media by such artists as Leonardo da Vinci, Titian, Raphael, Monet, Rubens, Rembrandt, and Rodin. The Smithsonian's Arthur M. Sackler Gallery *(p81)* has an exceptional collection of Asian artwork, including ancient Chinese jade and bronze, while the National Museum of African Art *(p81)* has some excellent examples of ancient African art on display.

←

Sculptures at the National Museum of African Art

Electronic Superhighway
(1995) at the Smithsonian
American Art Museum

TOP 5 MUST-SEE MUSEUMS

National Gallery of Art
World-class European and American art *(p66)*.

The Phillips Collection
America's first museum of modern art *(p150)*.

The SAAM
One of DC's favorite art museums *(p92)*.

Arthur M. Sackler Gallery
Contemporary and ancient Asian art *(p81)*.

National Museum of African Art
The first US museum for African art *(p81)*.

Modern and Contemporary

The Phillips Collection *(p150)* boasts art by Renoir, O'Keefe, Klee, and Rothko. Edgy, innovative, and unique art is on display at the Hirshhorn Museum *(p81)*, while the National Gallery of Art showcases works by artists such as Miró, Moore, and Calder.

→

Renoir's *Luncheon of the Boating Party* (1881), Phillips Collection

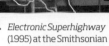

Performing Arts

One of the nation's busiest performing arts centers, the Kennedy Center *(p115)* in Georgetown features top music, dance, and theatrical events on its nine stages. To experience cutting-edge, experimental performances in an intimate setting, head to the Woolly Mammoth Theatre on D Street in Penn Quarter, while the best of Broadway is available at the National Theatre *(p99)*.

→

Bust of John F. Kennedy at the Kennedy Center

Mini Memorials

Spend a fun day locating and enjoying some of DC's dozens of lesser-known memorials. The warm, inviting figure of Einstein in front of the National Academy of Sciences at 22nd St and Constitution Avenue, NW is popular with children, who like to climb up into his lap. The George Mason Memorial at the Tidal Basin is a lovely spot with gardens, a fountain, and a statue of a relaxed Mason sitting on a bench. Mason became known as the forgotten Founding Father because he played a large role in crafting the new Constitution but refused to sign it as, among other things, it did not end the slave trade. The Titanic Memorial on the Southwest waterfront at P Street, SW was erected by the surviving women passengers to honor the men who stayed behind.

→

Enjoying climbing up the Albert Einstein Memorial

WASHINGTON, DC
OFF THE BEATEN PATH

Washington, DC has so many world-renowned attractions that some smaller sites get overlooked. All gems in their own right, they tell important stories, like the forgotten Founding Father, why George Washington kept a distillery, or the grisly but inspiring history of military medicine.

Hidden History

Some small sites tell big stories. In Silver Spring, Maryland, the National Museum of Health and Medicine focuses on the study of anatomic anomalies, medical curiosities, and military injuries. Washington's distillery at Mount Vernon (p162) was once his most successful business. Along with the neighboring gristmill, it has been rebuilt, and visitors can watch whiskey being made as it was in Washington's day.

Did You Know?

With dinner at the Inn at Mount Vernon, you can taste whiskeys from Washington's distillery.

↑ George Washington's distillery, Mount Vernon

← Guided tours taking in the displays at the National Museum of Health and Medicine

It's All in the Timing

Sometimes it's not about where, but when. A stroll around the west end of the National Mall (p62) after twilight, when all the paths and monuments are beautifully lit, is a little-known treat for visitors. On some balmy summer evenings, there are free movies shown on giant open-air screens near the Washington Monument (p82). Across town, the H Street Corridor (p100) is one of the city's trendiest after-dark venues, offering creative dining and great entertainment and nightlife.

← The World War II Memorial, Washington Monument, and the National Mall illuminated at night

TOP 5 LITTLE-KNOWN SITES

Heurich House
⊙ E4 ⌂ 1307 New Hampshire Ave NW ⒲ heurichhouse.org
Home of 19th-century city brewmaster Christian Heurich.

Khalil Gibran Memorial
⊙ C2 ⌂ 3100 Massachusetts Ave NW
A garden dedicated to the poet and philosopher.

The Awakening
National Harbor sculpture emerging from the earth (p173).

Mansion on O Street
⊙ E4 ⌂ 2020 O St NW
Eclectic mansion with secret passages.

DEA Museum
⊙ P4 ⌂ 700 Army Navy Dr
Arlington museum on the history of drug enforcement.

WASHINGTON, DC FOR
FAMILIES

With museums packed with cool stuff, scores of parks, and space to run, play, and fly kites on the National Mall, Washington, DC is one of the best cities in the US for kids to learn about the history of the country, be exposed to the most advanced science and technology in the world, and just have fun.

Just Plain Fun

In National Harbor (p173), The Awakening, a statue of a giant emerging from the earth, is popular with youngsters, who climb all over it. Nearby, the Capital Wheel whisks them 180 ft (55 m) above the river for thrills and incredible views. Another favorite is the International Spy Museum (p140), where kids create cover stories and become a spy for a day. And at the end of the day, a paddleboat ride around the Tidal Basin (p84) is a great way to wind down.

$\rightarrow$

Kids having fun at the International Spy Museum

The Greatest Outdoors

The National Zoo (p170) is a huge, park-like space that just happens to have giraffes, pandas, and thousands of other animals, all in natural enclosures. The National Arboretum (p172) is a vast garden with a great tram tour and places to let off steam while learning about trees. And nothing is better than flying a kite on the National Mall near the Washington Monument (p82) – breezy spring and fall are best, and kites are available in most museum gift shops.

←

Visitors touring the National Arboretum, and flying kites on the National Mall (inset)

TOP 5 MORE GREAT TIMES FOR KIDS

National Museum of American History
Treasure trove of Americana including Kermit the Frog (p76).

Oxon Hill Farm
Great for feeding farm animals and learning about rural life (p173).

Canal Boat Tour
Boat trips start from the Great Falls Visitor Center (p184).

Bike and Bus Tours
Rides on open-top tour buses (p196), and bikes on the National Mall.

Ice Cream
Try Larry's Homemade Ice Cream (www.larrys icecreamdc.com).

The Coolest History

Washington, DC has some of the biggest and most exciting museums in the US. First on the list is the Museum of Natural History (p74), where kids can handle giant bugs and gaze into the toothy grin of a Tyrannosaurus rex at the David H. Koch Hall of Fossils. The nearby Air and Space Museum (p70), home to the first television model of the Enterprise, also has wow-power. Mount Vernon (p162) offers a fun horse-drawn wagon ride around Pioneer Farm.

↑ Diplodocus exhibit at the National Museum of Natural History

↑ Magnificently decorated interior of the Library of Congress

Tour America's Government

Many of Washington, DC's beautiful government build-ings are filled with historical significance and amazing art, and are open to visitors for free tours. These include the National Archives *(p96)*, the United States Capitol *(p54)*, the White House *(p108)*, and the Library of Congress *(p59)*, the world's largest archive.

WASHINGTON, DC
ON A SHOESTRING

Washington, DC's amazing variety of free attractions ensures that visitors will never run out of things to see and do. Free museums, tours, and green spaces keep visitors active during the day, while theater and film festivals and music performances make evenings a delight.

 FREE SIGHTS

US Capitol
Grand space with the Brumidi Corridors and a stunning rotunda *(p54)*.

The National Mall and Memorial Parks
DC's central feature, with several memorials and monuments *(p82)*.

National Gallery of Art
One of the most visited galleries in the US *(p66)*.

Smithsonian Museums
A collection of 18 fascinating museums and galleries *(p70)*.

National Archives
Home to the nation's most important histor-ical documents *(p96)*.

Festivals and Events

The capital is packed with an incredible variety of free festivals and events. There are regular performances on the Millennium Stage at the Kennedy Center *(p115)*, ranging from comedy and the spoken word to dance and all forms of music. The National Gallery of Art *(p66)* holds the open-air Jazz in the Garden series every Friday in summer, while the DC Jazz Festival *(p40)* includes free concerts alongside ticketed ones. The Shakespeare Theatre Company's Free For All *(p41)* is a much-loved city tradition, offering performances of the Bard's works each summer. Foodies will enjoy the free tastings at the Giant National Capital Barbecue Battle in June, while film buffs can choose between the NoMa CiNoMatic, an outdoor movie series in Alethia Tanner Park, and Films at the Stone, screened at the Martin Luther King, Jr. Memorial.

$\rightarrow$
Band performing at the DC Jazz Festival

Gardens, Galleries, and Museums

Washington, DC is a city filled with glorious green spaces, magnificent art, and amazing artifacts. The US Botanic Garden *(p58)* offers serene beauty, while the National Arboretum *(p172)* has breathtaking azalea gardens. On rainy days head indoors to the National Gallery of Art, the Smithsonian's 18 acclaimed museums, or any of the dozens of other world-class government and private museums that are free to enter and guaranteed to engross.

↑ Robert Indiana's *AMOR* at the National Gallery of Art *(inset)*, and the US Botanic Garden

A YEAR IN
WASHINGTON, DC

JANUARY

△ **Restaurant Week** (*mid-Jan*). Many of the city's top restaurants offer fixed-price specials for lunch or dinner.

Martin Luther King, Jr. Day (*3rd Mon*). Commemorative events are held at the Martin Luther King, Jr. Memorial, Washington National Cathedral, Kennedy Center, and others.

FEBRUARY

Black History Month (*throughout*). Theater, dance, music, visual arts, and spoken-word events.

△ **Chinese New Year** (*1st two weeks*). Enjoy parades, dancing, and live music at N St, Chinatown.

Presidents' Day Weekend (*3rd Mon*). All past presidents are honored at multiple events, such as the George Washington Birthday Parade.

MAY

Washington National Cathedral Flower Mart (*1st Fri*). Flower and gift booths and music on offer.

Around the World Embassy Tour (*1st Sat*). Over 40 embassies welcome visitors and provide cultural events and experiences.

△ **Memorial Day** (*last Mon*). Wreath-laying, speeches, and music honor war veterans at city memorials and Arlington National Cemetery.

JUNE

△ **Capital Pride** (*early Jun*). A street festival and parade celebrate the LGBTQ+ communities of DC.

DC Jazz Festival (*mid-Jun*). This two-week festival attracts the best musicians from across the US.

Smithsonian Folklife Festival (*late Jun–early Jul*). This huge celebration of folk culture includes music, dance, games, and food on the National Mall.

SEPTEMBER

△ **Labor Day Weekend Concert** (*Sun before Labor Day*). The National Symphony Orchestra performs on the West Lawn of the Capitol.

H Street Festival (*mid-Sep*). This spirited block party offers food booths, art, and performances on 14 stages.

Fiesta DC (*late Sep*). A colorful parade and festival celebrate Latino culture.

OCTOBER

△ **Annapolis Boat Shows** (*mid-Oct*). World's largest sailboat and powerboat shows with in-water boat access, workshops, and exhibits.

White House Fall Garden Tours (*mid-Oct*). Visits to the Rose Garden, Jacqueline Kennedy Garden, Children's Garden, and the South Lawn are on offer.

Boo at the Zoo (*end Oct*). A Halloween celebration for children at the National Zoo with treats, education, and live entertainment.

MARCH

St. Patrick's Day *(Sun before Mar 17)*. A parade to celebrate Irish culture on Constitution Avenue, NW.

△ **Blossom Kite Festival** *(last Sat)*. Kite enthusiasts gather near the Washington Monument on the National Mall to fly their kites and compete for prizes.

National Cherry Blossom Festival *(late Mar–mid-Apr)*. A parade and festivities celebrate the blooming of Washington's famous cherry trees.

APRIL

△ **White House Easter Egg Roll** *(Easter Mon)*. Children's egg races and entertainment.

Truckeroo *(Apr–Sep)*. This one-Friday-a-month food truck event also features live music.

Filmfest DC *(late Apr–early May)*. New films from around the world plus film-oriented events.

JULY

Military Band Concert Series *(Jun–Aug)*. Free concerts are held at the Capitol and military memorials on most evenings.

△ **Independence Day** *(Jul 4)*. A free concert at the Capitol, a parade along Constitution Avenue, and fireworks on the National Mall. Old Town Alexandria and Mount Vernon have parades and fireworks.

Capital Fringe Festival *(last 3 weeks)*. More than 100 independent theater, dance, music, art, and other live performances take place.

AUGUST

△ **Arlington County Fair** *(mid-Aug)*. A lively fair with food, crafts, music, and fairground rides.

Summer Restaurant Week *(mid-Aug)*. More than 250 restaurants offer fixed-price dinners, brunches, and lunches.

Free for All *(late Aug–early Sep)*. This popular annual summer event sees free nightly performances of the Bard's classic plays by the Shakespeare Theatre Company.

NOVEMBER

Veterans Day *(Nov 11)*. Wreath-laying, services, and concerts take place at Arlington National Cemetery and various city memorials to honor veterans.

△ **Sculpture Garden Ice Rink** *(mid-Nov–Mar)*. The pond at the National Gallery of Art's Sculpture Garden becomes a popular ice rink each winter.

Kennedy Center Holiday Festival *(late Nov–New Year's Eve)*. Enjoy musicals, ballet, and classical concerts for the holiday season.

DECEMBER

ZooLights *(late Nov–Jan 1)*. Thousands of light sculptures portray the popular animals, alongside activities and live entertainment.

Christmas at Mount Vernon *(late Nov–early Jan)*. Experience an 18th-century Christmas at Mount Vernon, George Washington's plantation.

△ **National Christmas Tree** *(throughout)*. The decorated National Christmas Tree, and 56 state and territory trees, stand in the Ellipse near the White House. Live entertainment nightly.

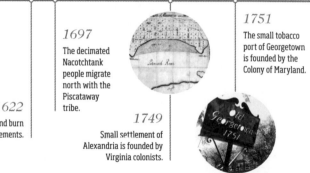

A BRIEF
HISTORY

Washington, DC was designed from the ground up to be the capital, with wide avenues, lush parks, and grand buildings. Over the years it has also been a thriving port, an urban fortress in the Civil War, a safe harbor for those fleeing slavery, and, after World War II, a flourishing center of arts and culture.

Before the Europeans

Native American civilizations have lived in the Washington, DC area for thousands of years. In 1608, English soldier John Smith was the first European to explore the trading settlements of the people of Nacotchtank village (or Anacostans), who lived along the banks of the Anacostia and Potomac rivers. In subsequent decades the Nacotchtank people, along with thousands of other Native Americans, died from diseases introduced by European settlers and from conflicts with the British colonies of Virginia and Maryland. By the time Alexandria and Georgetown were founded in the mid-1700s, the Nacotchtank people had long been driven out.

1 An old map of the city.

2 John Hancock holding the signed US Declaration of Independence.

3 George Washington receiving the news of his election as the first American president.

4 British troops setting fire to the city during the War of 1812.

Timeline of events

1608
The Nacotchtank people are visited by Captain John Smith.

1622
The British raid and burn Nacotchtank settlements.

1697
The decimated Nacotchtank people migrate north with the Piscataway tribe.

1749
Small settlement of Alexandria is founded by Virginia colonists.

1751
The small tobacco port of Georgetown is founded by the Colony of Maryland.

A New City

America declared its independence from Great Britain in 1776, and after emerging victorious in the Revolutionary War (1775–83), elected George Washington as the nation's first president in 1789. In return for agreeing to Alexander Hamilton's plan for the national government to take on the states' Revolutionary War debts, Thomas Jefferson and James Madison secured the federal capital on territory bridging the northern and southern states, along the Potomac River. Washington selected the exact site on mostly empty land to the east of Georgetown shortly after, and asked his old friend Major Pierre Charles L'Enfant to create a grand city plan (p85). In 1800, the US government officially moved from Philadelphia to what was now called the city of Washington, DC.

The City Burns

The US and Britain fought again in the War of 1812. The war ended in a stalemate in 1815, but a year before that, British forces had set fire to numerous buildings, partially destroying the White House and the US Capitol. Rebuilding was swift and the arrival of the railroad in 1835 gave the city a further boost.

Did You Know?

George Washington died before the White House was finished so John Adams was the first president to live in it.

1776
The American colonies declare their independence from Great Britain.

1790
The Compromise of 1790 locates the new national capital on the Potomac.

1800
The Federal government moves from Philadelphia to Washington, DC.

1814
The British set fire to Washington, DC during the War of 1812.

Slavery and the Civil War

Over the next few decades, the city reflected the nation's growing tensions over slavery and Alexandria developed into a major slave trade market. The Compromise of 1850 outlawed the slave trade in Washington, DC, though not slavery itself. In 1860, following the presidential election of Abraham Lincoln, many southern states seceded from the Union, launching the Civil War a year later. Washington, DC became a giant military camp, but the city never fell to the Confederacy. Slavery was finally abolished in DC in 1862 – eight months before Lincoln's Emancipation Proclamation. The war ended with Union victory in 1865, but disaffected Confederate actor John Wilkes Booth assassinated Lincoln soon after at Ford's Theatre. Development of the city remained sluggish, and it wasn't until the 1890s that Washington, DC formally absorbed Georgetown.

A New Century

In 1901, participation in the City Beautiful movement led to massive urban development and a huge advance for L'Enfant's grand plan. When the US entered World War I in 1917, women came to the city to fill the posts vacated by men, and suffragists

CAMP WASHINGTON

On April 12, 1861, shots were fired on Fort Sumter and the Civil War began. By summer, 50,000 army volunteers had arrived in Washington, DC, and the city found itself in the business of housing, feeding, and clothing them, as well as caring for the wounded. Among those who came to help were author Louisa May Alcott and poet Walt Whitman.

Timeline of events

1861
The Civil War begins.

1862
Slavery is abolished in the city.

1865
Union victory in the Civil War; President Lincoln is assassinated at Ford's Theatre.

1867
General Oliver Otis Howard helps establish the African American Howard University.

1877
The *Washington Post* newspaper is founded.

took to the streets to campaign for women's right to vote. The war also saw the start of the Great Migration, the movement of millions of African Americans out of the rural South. Though segregation continued in DC, with African Americans banned from voting and discriminated against in housing and education, thousands came to take up better paying jobs in the city. As a result, the 1920s were a period of commercial, artistic, and literary success for the Black community, with the area around U Street attracting creative African Americans.

The New Deal and World War II

Following the stock market crash of 1929, President Roosevelt created the New Deal, an ambitious program that paid people to undertake public work, from planting trees on the National Mall to completing city buildings such as the National Gallery of Art and the Supreme Court. The March on Washington Movement, led by civil rights activist A. Philip Randolph, attempted to tackle the ongoing issue of segregation. After the US entered World War II in 1941, Washington's population soared. Once again, women from all across the country arrived in the capital, eager to take on government jobs while the men were overseas.

[1] John Wilkes Booth shooting Abraham Lincoln in 1865.

[2] Suffragists inviting people to protest, 1917.

[3] National Gallery of Art being built, 1939.

[4] Traders crowding the New York Stock Exchange trading floor during the stock market crash of 1929.

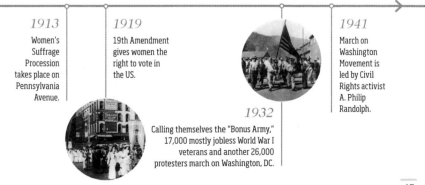

1913
Women's Suffrage Procession takes place on Pennsylvania Avenue.

1919
19th Amendment gives women the right to vote in the US.

1932
Calling themselves the "Bonus Army," 17,000 mostly jobless World War I veterans and another 26,000 protesters march on Washington, DC.

1941
March on Washington Movement is led by Civil Rights activist A. Philip Randolph.

1

2

Civil Rights and a New Beginning

The Great Migration continued to bring African Americans to DC and in 1957, it became the first major city in the US with a majority Black population. Yet living conditions in much of the city remained very poor. After the Supreme Court passed anti-discrimination laws, Washington, DC gradually desegregated in the 1950s. On August 28, 1963, Martin Luther King, Jr. led the March on Washington to support civil rights, and from the steps of the Lincoln Memorial shared his dream (p101). In the aftermath of the shock assassination of Dr. King in 1968, DC was rocked by four days of riots. "White flight" to the suburbs accelerated, leaving parts of the city underfunded and undeveloped.

Into the Modern Era

Popular civil rights activist Marion Barry became mayor of DC in 1978. By the late 1980s the US crack epidemic was becoming a massive problem in DC, and by 1990 the city had the highest homicide rate in the nation. Sharon Pratt Kelly was the first Black woman to become mayor of a US city from 1991 to 1995. By the end of the 1990s, DC had regained a measure of financial and social stability. Nevertheless, the terrorist attacks on

Did You Know?

Theodore Roosevelt was shot at in 1912, but the bullet was slowed by a 50-page speech in his coat pocket.

Timeline of events

1968
Riots break out and blocks of Washington, DC are burned following the assassination of Dr. King.

1971
The *Washington Post* publishes the Pentagon Papers.

1975
Walter Washington becomes the first elected and first Black mayor of the city.

1976
The DC Metro opens with just one route, five stations, and 4.6 miles (7.5 km) of track. Today, it has six routes, 91 stations, and 117 miles (188 km) of track.

2014
Marijuana is legalized in the District of Columbia.

September 11, 2001, on New York and Washington, DC forever altered life in the US capital, creating a heightened need for security that is still felt by residents and visitors alike today.

Washington, DC Today

In 2009, Barack Obama became the first African American president in US history; in 2015, Muriel Bowser became mayor of DC, the second Black woman to hold the job. Yet events in the city continue to reflect major divisions across the US. The inauguration of President Donald Trump in 2017 was followed by the Women's March, the largest single-day protest in US history. Black Lives Matter protests rocked the capital in 2020 after the murder of George Floyd, and in 2021 supporters of Donald Trump attempted to seize the US Capitol to stop his succession by Joe Biden. One burning issue remains for DC itself – statehood. It is the only part of the US without representation in Congress. A statehood bill passed in the House in 2020 has been stalled in the Senate – for now. The 51st state is slated to be called the "State of Washington, Douglass Commonwealth" to honor Frederick Douglass, the 19th-century leader of the abolitionist movement (p172), who spent much of his time in Washington, DC.

1 Dr. King at the 1963 March on Washington. ↑

2 Democratic mayoral nominee Marion Barry, (left) as he leaves a fire fighters convention in Washington, DC in September, 1978.

3 The George Floyd Memorial at George Floyd Square, Washington, DC.

4 President Joe Biden and Vice President Kamala Harris during a Democratic primary debate before the presidential election.

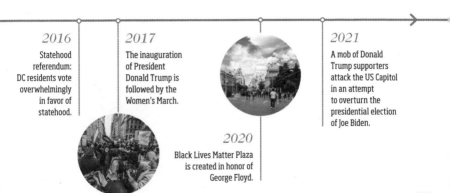

2016
Statehood referendum: DC residents vote overwhelmingly in favor of statehood.

2017
The inauguration of President Donald Trump is followed by the Women's March.

2020
Black Lives Matter Plaza is created in honor of George Floyd.

2021
A mob of Donald Trump supporters attack the US Capitol in an attempt to overturn the presidential election of Joe Biden.

EXPERIENCE

YRANNY OVER THE MIN

I AM NOT AN ADVOCATE FOR FREQU
CHANGES IN LAWS AND CONSTITUT
BUT LAWS AND INSTITUTIONS MUS
HAND IN HAND WITH THE PROG
OF THE HUMAN MIND. AS THAT BEC
MORE DEVELOPED, MORE ENLIGHTE
AS NEW DISCOVERIES ARE MADE
TRUTHS DISCOVERED AND MANNERS
OPINIONS CHANGE, WITH THE CH
OF CIRCUMSTANCES, INSTITUT
MUST ADVANCE ALSO TO KEEP
WITH THE TIMES. WE MIGHT AS
REQUIRE A MAN TO WEAR STILL
COAT WHICH FITTED HIM WHEN A
AS CIVILIZED SOCIETY TO REM
EVER UNDER THE REGIMEN OF T
BARBAROUS ANCESTORS.

CAPITOL HILL

The Piscataway, Pamunkey, Nentego (Nanichoke), Mattaponi, Chickahominy, Monacan, and Powhatan peoples originally lived along the banks of the Anacostia and Potomac rivers, including on land that is today occupied by Washington DC's Capitol Hill neighborhood. For centuries these peoples had a thriving culture until the arrival of European settlers in the late 1600s, who drove away the Indigenous populations in order to appropriate their land and brought with them new diseases, which decimated the local populations.

In 1791 President Washington chose a site along the banks of the Anacostia and Potomac rivers for the capital of the United States and appointed the engineer and architect Pierre Charles L'Enfant to plan the new city of Washington. L'Enfant selected a hill in the east of the area for the seat of the Capitol building, which was to house the United States Congress, the law-making branch of the US government. The first section of the building was completed by 1800, when Congress officially took up residence. The US Capitol was expanded in the 1850s, and its famous cast-iron dome was completed by 1866. The area surrounding the US Capitol boomed after the US Civil War in the late 19th century and has remained a somewhat affluent district of late Victorian homes ever since, with further gentrification since the 1990s.

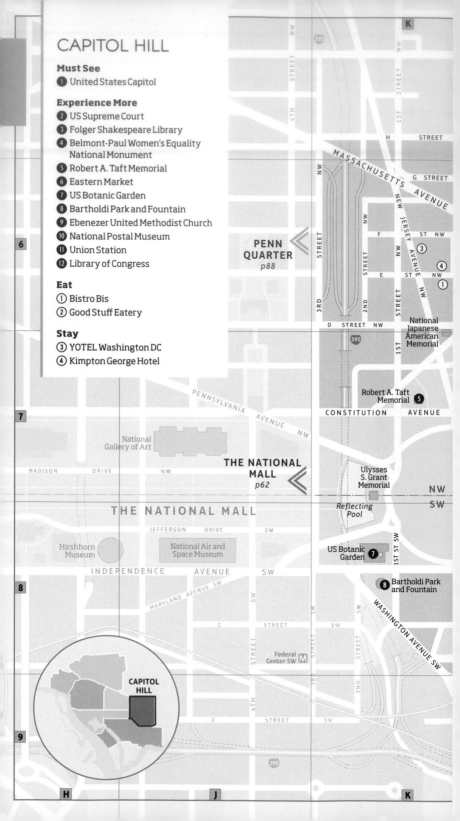

CAPITOL HILL

Must See
① United States Capitol

Experience More
② US Supreme Court
③ Folger Shakespeare Library
④ Belmont-Paul Women's Equality National Monument
⑤ Robert A. Taft Memorial
⑥ Eastern Market
⑦ US Botanic Garden
⑧ Bartholdi Park and Fountain
⑨ Ebenezer United Methodist Church
⑩ National Postal Museum
⑪ Union Station
⑫ Library of Congress

Eat
① Bistro Bis
② Good Stuff Eatery

Stay
③ YOTEL Washington DC
④ Kimpton George Hotel

PENN QUARTER p88

National Japanese American Memorial

Robert A. Taft Memorial ⑤

CONSTITUTION   AVENUE

PENNSYLVANIA   AVENUE NW

National Gallery of Art

THE NATIONAL MALL p62

MADISON   DRIVE   NW

Ulysses S. Grant Memorial

NW
SW

Reflecting Pool

THE NATIONAL MALL

JEFFERSON   DRIVE   SW

Hirshhorn Museum

National Air and Space Museum

US Botanic Garden ⑦   1ST ST SW

INDEPENDENCE   AVENUE   SW

MARYLAND AVENUE SW

⑧ Bartholdi Park and Fountain

WASHINGTON AVENUE SW

C   STREET   SW

Federal Center SW Ⓜ

CAPITOL HILL

E   STREET   SW

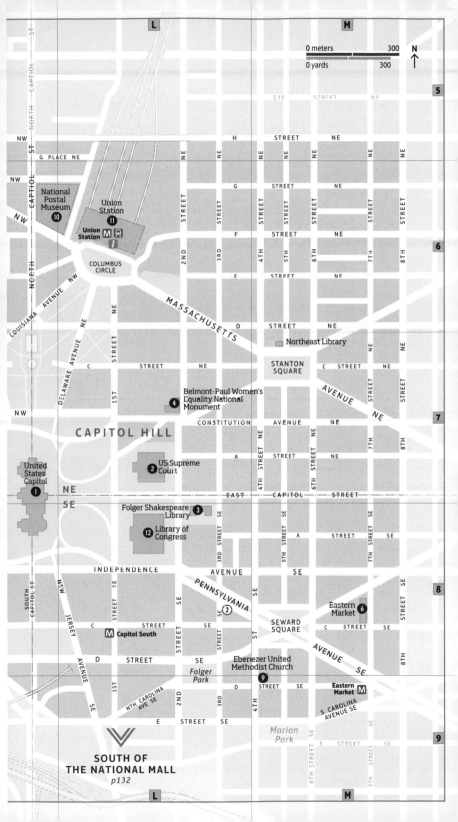

① Ⓜ Ⓨ Ⓐ

UNITED STATES CAPITOL

📍K7 🚪Main entrance: beneath East Front Plaza at 1st & East Capitol Sts Ⓜ Capitol South, Union Station, Federal Center SW 🚌32, 34, 36, 96 🕐8:30am–4:30pm Mon–Sat (check website for details) 🚫Federal hols Ⓦ visitthecapitol.gov

The Capitol is one of the world's best-known symbols of democracy. Every year about four million visitors come to admire the breathtaking building and learn how America creates and passes the laws that govern the nation.

Since 1793, when George Washington laid the cornerstone, the Neo-Classical Capitol has been under almost constant renovation. In 2008 the vast visitor center opened, welcoming visitors to the building's stunning interior, with its vaulted ceilings, exquisite tile- and woodwork, and expansive art-filled spaces. While waiting for a free tour (book ahead up to 90 days in advance), visitors can explore the Exhibition Hall, where artifacts and original documents tell the story of Congress and the Capitol Building. There are also videos, models, and interactive computers, as well as two theaters showing the proceedings in the House and Senate Chambers. The Emancipation Hall honors the enslaved laborers who helped build the Capitol building.

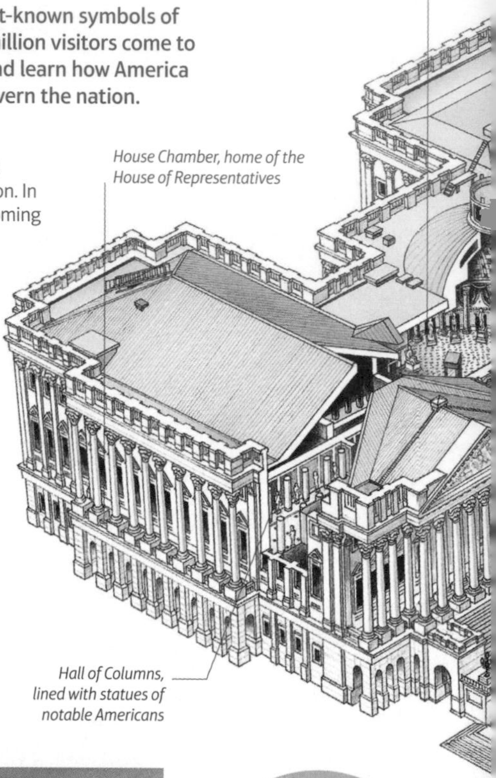

National Statuary Hall, with two statues from each state

House Chamber, home of the House of Representatives

→
The United States Capitol building, the legislative heart of Washington, DC

Hall of Columns, lined with statues of notable Americans

Did You Know?

When the two Chambers of Congress are in session, the viewing galleries are open to the public.

←
The Capitol, marking the center of the city, whose quadrants are defined by a point directly below the building's dome

Cast-iron dome, originally built of wood and copper

The 180-ft- (55-m-) high Rotunda, capped by Brumidi's fresco The Apotheosis of Washington

Senate Chamber, home of the US Senate since 1859

Brumidi Corridors

Old Senate Chamber, occupied by the Senate until 1859, then by the Supreme Court until 1934

Columbus Doors, made of solid bronze

Crypt, with a central star denoting the city's quadrants

→

The Brumidi Corridors, decorated with frescoes, bronzes, and paintings by Italian artist Constantino Brumidi (1805–80)

1791
△ George Washington selects the site for the Capitol; later, William Thornton wins a contest to design the building.

1814
△ During the War of 1812 the British burn part of the Capitol; it is again damaged by fire in 1851 and 1898.

1958
△ A major expansion of the Capitol building starts with a 32-ft (10-m) extension of the east front.

2021
△ Former president Trump's supporters storm the Capitol, attempting to overturn his electoral defeat; five people die.

EXPERIENCE MORE

②

US Supreme Court

📍L7 🏛1st St between E Capitol St & Maryland Ave, NE Ⓜ Capitol South 🕐9am–4:30pm Mon–Fri 🚫Federal hols 🌐supremecourt.gov

Emblazoned with the motto "Equal Justice Under Law," this elegant Corinthian building was designed by Cass Gilbert and opened in 1935. Sculptures depicting the allegorical figures of the *Contemplation of Justice* and the *Guardian of the Law* stand beside the steps while above the entrance are figures of John Marshall (far right) and William Howard Taft (far left), the fourth and tenth US Chief Justices, respectively.

The Supreme Court forms the judicial and third branch of the US government,

> 💬 INSIDER TIP
> **Legal Drama**
>
> To watch the Supreme Court in action, arrive well before the 9:30am seating and pick either the queue for a full one-hour argument (this line forms days in advance; only the first 50 get in) or for a three-minute slot.

providing the highest ruling in the nation's legal disputes and issues of constitutionality. All oral arguments are open to the public, but admission is on a first-come, first-served basis, and seating is limited. When not in session, public lectures on the court are held every hour on the half-hour in the courtroom (check details on the website). In addition to the courtroom, portions of the first and ground floors are open to the public.

---

③

Folger Shakespeare Library

📍L8 🏛201 E Capitol St, SE Ⓜ Capitol South 🕐For renovation until 2023; check website for latest information 🌐folger.edu

Housing the world's largest collection of Shakespeare's printed works, this library and museum celebrate the writings of the Elizabethan playwright.

The research library was a gift to the American people in 1932 from Henry Clay Folger who, as a student in 1874,

began to collect Shakespeare's works. Folger funded the construction of this edifice, built specifically to house his collection. It contains 310,000 Elizabethan books and manuscripts, including 82 copies of the 1623 First Folio (the first complete collection of the Bard's plays printed after his death), and 200 quartos (pamphlets of individual Shakespeare plays printed during his lifetime).

The Folger hosts cultural events such as regular performances of the Bard's plays in a 250-seat reconstruction of an Elizabethan theater.

---

④

Belmont-Paul Women's Equality National Monument

📍L7 🏛144 Constitution Ave, NE Ⓜ Capitol South, Union Station 🕐9am–5pm Wed–Sun 🚫Federal hols 🌐nps.gov/bepa

A stately historic home, this is also a museum dedicated to the story of the women's suffrage and equal rights

→ The imposing Neo-Classical facade of the US Supreme Court

→ A kaleidoscopic display of some of the fresh produce on offer at Eastern Market

movements. Between 1929 and 2021 (when the party ceased operations), it was the headquarters of the National Women's Party, who won the right for American women to vote in 1920. Today, visitors can admire the period furnishings and suffragist artifacts, including the desk on which Alice Paul, the leader of the party, wrote the still unratified Equal Rights Amendment of 1923.

A century earlier, in the early 1800s, the house was the home of Albert Gallatin, the Treasury Secretary under President Thomas Jefferson. It was here that Gallatin entertained a number of wealthy contributors whose financial backing brought about the Louisiana Purchase in 1803, which doubled the size of the United States.

5

Robert A. Taft Memorial

📍 K7 🏛 Constitution Ave & 1st St, NW Ⓜ Union Station 🌐 aoc.gov

In a park opposite the US Capitol stands this statue of Ohio senator Robert A. Taft (1889–1953). The son of the 27th US president William Howard Taft, Robert was a Republican, famous for

sponsoring the Taft-Hartley Act, the regulator of collective bargaining between labor and management. The memorial, designed by Douglas W. Orr, was erected in 1959 as a "tribute to the honesty, indomitable courage, and high principles of free government symbolized by his life." The 10-ft- (3-m-) tall bronze statue, by American sculptor Wheeler Williams, is dwarfed by a 100-ft- (30-m-) high, white Tennessee marble bell tower (the Carillon) that rises up behind the figure of the politician.

🔥 💻 🏛

Eastern Market

📍 M8 🏛 7th & C Sts, SE Ⓜ Eastern Market 🕐 7am–7pm Tue-Fri, 7am-6pm Sat, 9am-5pm Sun 🚫 Jan 1, Jul 4, Thanksgiving, Dec 25 & 26 🌐 easternmarket-dc.org

This block-long market hall has been a fixture in Capitol Hill since 1871, and the provisions sold today still have an Old World flavor. Big beef steaks and fresh pigs' feet are everywhere, along with gourmet sausages and cheeses from all over the world. The aroma of fresh bread, roasted chicken, and flowers pervades the hall. On Friday afternoons, Saturdays, and Sundays the covered stalls outside are filled with crafts and farmers' produce;

on Sundays these popular stalls also host a flea market. The market was designed by local architect Adolph Cluss. Destroyed in a fire in 2007, it has been rebuilt with modern interiors that retain their old charm. Along with Union Market north of the Capitol, it is one of the few public markets left in Washington that are still used for their original purpose.

EAT

Bistro Bis
Breakfast at this upscale French bistro is one of the best places in DC to spot celebrities and Congressional power brokers. Lunch and dinner are equally creative and rewarding.

📍 K6 🏛 15 E St, NW 🌐 bistrobis.com

💲💲💲

Good Stuff Eatery
American classics such as burgers, fries, and milkshakes are all lovingly handmade from farm-fresh ingredients.

📍 L8 🏛 303 Pennsylvania Ave, SE 🌐 goodstuffeatery.com

💲💲💲

← Bartholdi Park, with its centerpiece fountain

a new church, Little Ebenezer, was built to take the overflow. After the 1863 Emancipation Proclamation, Congress ruled that Black children should receive public education. In 1864, Little Ebenezer became DC's first school for Black children. The number of members grew steadily and another church was built in 1868, but was damaged by a storm in 1896. The replacement, built in 1897, is Ebenezer United Methodist Church. A model of Little Ebenezer stands outside.

7 US Botanic Garden

⦿ K8 ⊞ Independence Ave & 1st St, SW; entrance at 100 Maryland Ave, SW Ⓜ Federal Center SW ⏱ Gardens: 7:30am-5pm daily (Apr-mid-Sep: to 7pm); conservatory: 10am-5pm daily ⊕ usbg.gov

This conservatory and garden near the southwest corner of the Capitol is a wonderful oasis for anyone seeking a restful interlude from the National Mall. The 80-ft- (24-m-) tall Palm House creates a venue for a jungle of tropical and subtropical plants. Other specialties are plants native to deserts in the Old and New Worlds, plants of economic and healing value, and endangered plants.

The Botanic Garden was established to cultivate plants that could be beneficial to the American people. It was revitalized in 1842, when the Wilkes Expedition to the South Seas brought back a variety of international plants, some of which are still on display.

A National Garden of plants native to the mid-Atlantic lies on 3 acres (1 ha) of land west of the conservatory. It includes a Water Garden, a Rose Garden, and a terraced lawn. Visitors can dial (202) 730-9303 from their smartphones to stream an audio tour as they walk through the garden.

8 Bartholdi Park and Fountain

⦿ K8 ⊞ Independence Ave & 1st St, SW Ⓜ Federal Center SW ⏱ Dawn-dusk daily ⊕ usbg.gov/bartholdi-park

The graceful, symmetrical fountain that dominates this park was created by Frédéric August Bartholdi (sculptor of the Statue of Liberty) for the Centennial Exposition of 1876, held in Philadelphia to mark the 100th anniversary of the signing of the Declaration of Independence. Originally lit by gas lamps, the Fountain of Light and Water was converted to electric lighting in 1881. Made of cast iron, it is adorned with nymph and triton figures, and has tiny model gardens planted around it. Areas in the park include therapeutic, romantic, and heritage plants, such as Virginia sneezeweed, Sweet William, and wild oats.

9 Ebenezer United Methodist Church

⦿ M9 ⊞ 4th & D Sts, SE Ⓜ Eastern Market ⏱ 10am-2pm Tue-Fri ⏱ Federal hols

Established in 1827, this was the first Black church to serve Methodists in Washington. Attendance grew rapidly, and

10 National Postal Museum

⦿ L6 ⊞ 2 Massachusetts Ave, NE Ⓜ Union Station ⏱ 10am-5:30pm daily ⏱ Dec 25 ⊕ postalmuseum. si.edu

Opened by the Smithsonian Institution in 1990, this fascinating museum is housed in the former City Post Office building. One of the centerpieces of the collection is the wood-and-fabric plane in which Sam Wiseman flew the first recorded airmail flight from Petaluma, California, to Santa Rosa in 1911. Other exhibits include a 1919 de Havilland DH4 biplane, the first official airmail service plane, along with a horse-drawn Concord Mail Coach and a postal rail car, showing how mail traveled before modern airmail.

The William H. Gross Stamp Gallery has one of the best collections in the world. "Binding the Nation" explains the history of US mail to the end of the 19th century. Other exhibits illustrate how the mail system works and how a stamp is created. At postcard kiosks, you can address a postcard electronically, see the route it will take, and drop it in a mailbox.

⑪ Union Station

📍 L6 🏛 50 Massachusetts Ave, NE Ⓜ Union Station 🕐 24 hours daily 🌐 unionstationdc.com

Spectacularly restored in 1988, the Beaux Arts Union Station offers visitors a potpourri of shops and restaurants, and a chance to stroll through one of the most dazzling architectural gems in the city.

When it was built in 1908, the elegant white granite structure with its three main archways, modeled on the Roman Arch of Constantine, was the largest train station in the world. For half a century, it remained a major transportation hub, but as air travel became increasingly popular, passenger trains went into decline. Restoration work began in 1981, and included embellishing the 96-ft- (29-m-) high ceiling, with 22-carat gold leaf. Today, Union Station is visited by more than 40 million people a year.

⑫ Library of Congress

📍 L8 🏛 101 Independence Ave, SE Ⓜ Capitol South 🕐 8:30am–4:30pm Mon-Sat ⊘ Jan 1, Thanksgiving, Dec 25 🌐 loc.gov

This palatial Italian Renaissance edifice is the hub of a network of stunning buildings that house the world's largest collection of books and other media. The library boasts an incredible 838 miles (1,349 km) of shelves that hold around 167 million items. Congress first established a reference library in the US Capitol in 1800. When the Capitol was burned down by the British in 1814, Jefferson sold his own collection to the government as a replacement, and his belief in a universality of knowledge became the foundation for the library's acquisition policy. Visitors can tour the grand main reading room, with its 160-ft- (49-m-) high dome, and see collection items that include a 15th-century Gutenberg Bible.

STAY

YOTEL Washington DC

This affordable boutique hotel has a great location near the Capitol, and boasts a rooftop pool and the trendy Art and Soul restaurant.

📍 K6 🏛 415 New Jersey Ave, NW 🌐 yotel.com

$$⑤

Kimpton George Hotel

Stylish and elegant, Kimpton George gets rave reviews for its sophisticated rooms and the excellent Bistro Bis (p57). The hotel offers complimentary wine hour and bicycles.

📍 K6 🏛 15 E St, NW 🌐 hotelgeorge.com

$$$

The desks in the Main Reading Room are dwarfed by eight huge marble columns and 10 ft (3 m) high female figures, personifying aspects of human endeavor.

This beautiful marble Mosaic of Minerva was created by Elihu Vedder.

The Gutenberg Bible was the first book printed using movable metal type. This is one of only three perfect vellum copies.

Asian Reading Room

The striking Neptune Fountain is in front of the Jefferson Building.

The African & Middle Eastern Reading Room is one of 10 reading rooms in the Jefferson Building.

Exhibition Area

Main Entrance

↑ The magnificent Library of Congress

A SHORT WALK
CAPITOL HILL

Distance 1.7 miles (2.7 km) **Nearest Metro** Capitol South
Time 35 minutes

The cityscape extending from the Capitol is an impressive combination of grand Classical architecture and stretches of grassy open spaces. There are no skyscrapers here, only the immense marble halls and columns that distinguish many of the government buildings. The bustle and excitement around the Capitol and Supreme Court contrast with the calm that can be found by the reflecting pool or in a quiet residential street. Many of the small touches that make the city special can be found in this area, such as the antique lighting fixtures on 2nd Street, the brilliant bursts of flowers along the sidewalks, or the brightly painted facades of the houses on 3rd Street near the Folger Shakespeare Library.

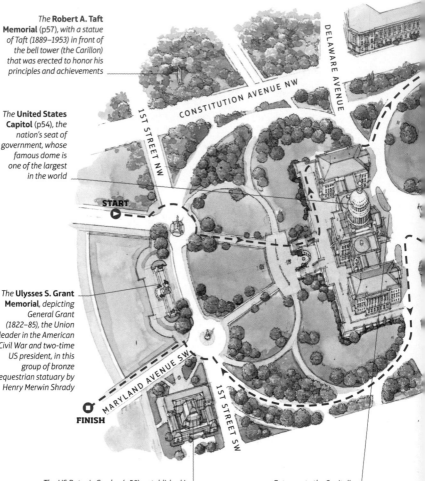

The **Robert A. Taft Memorial** (p57), with a statue of Taft (1889–1953) in front of the bell tower (the Carillon) that was erected to honor his principles and achievements

The **United States Capitol** (p54), the nation's seat of government, whose famous dome is one of the largest in the world

START

The **Ulysses S. Grant Memorial**, depicting General Grant (1822–85), the Union leader in the American Civil War and two-time US president, in this group of bronze equestrian statuary by Henry Merwin Shrady

FINISH

DELAWARE AVENUE

CONSTITUTION AVENUE NW

1ST STREET NW

MARYLAND AVENUE SW

1ST STREET SW

The US Botanic Garden (p58), established in 1820 and containing about 65,000 plants in a grand conservatory with ten habitats

Entrance to the Capitol's underground visitor center, located to the east of the building

Locator Map
For more detail see p52

↑ The front facade of the
US Supreme Court building

Senate Offices

CONSTITUTION AVENUE NE

MARYLAND AVENUE NE

2ND STREET NE

1ST STREET NE

EAST CAPITOL STREET

1ST STREET SE

2ND STREET SE

The **Belmont-Paul Women's Equality National Monument** (p56), *an 18th-century house that once served as the headquarters of the National Women's Party and has a life-size statue of the French saint Joan of Arc (a replica of a French sculpture) in the main hall*

The **US Supreme Court** (p56), *the highest court in the land, housed since 1935 in this Neo-Classical marble building with a portico of Corinthian columns designed by Cass Gilbert*

The **Folger Shakespeare Library** (p56), *containing the world's largest collection of historic Shakespeare texts and rare Renaissance materials*

The **Library of Congress** (p58), *which purchased Thomas Jefferson's personal book collection after the British had burned the original library using the books as kindling*

0 meters 150
0 yards 150

N ↑

→ The ornate
interior of the
Library of Congress

THE NATIONAL MALL

In L'Enfant's original plan for the new capital of the United States, the National Mall was conceived as a grand boulevard lined with diplomatic residences of elegant, Parisian-style architecture. L'Enfant's plan was never fully realized, but it is nevertheless a moving sight – this grand, tree-lined expanse is bordered on either side by the Smithsonian museums and features the Capitol at its eastern end and the Lincoln Memorial at its western end. This dramatic formal version of the National Mall did not materialize until after World War II. Until then the space was used for everything from a zoo to a railroad terminal to a wood yard. Today, the National Mall forms a vital part of the history of the United States. Innumerable demonstrators have gathered at the Lincoln Memorial and marched to the US Capitol. Pope John Paul II said Mass, African American soprano Marian Anderson sang at the request of first lady Eleanor Roosevelt, and Dr. Martin Luther King, Jr. delivered his famous "I Have a Dream" speech here. On summer evenings, teams of locals play softball and soccer on its fields, and every year, on the Fourth of July (Independence Day), America's birthday party is held on the National Mall with a spectacular fireworks display.

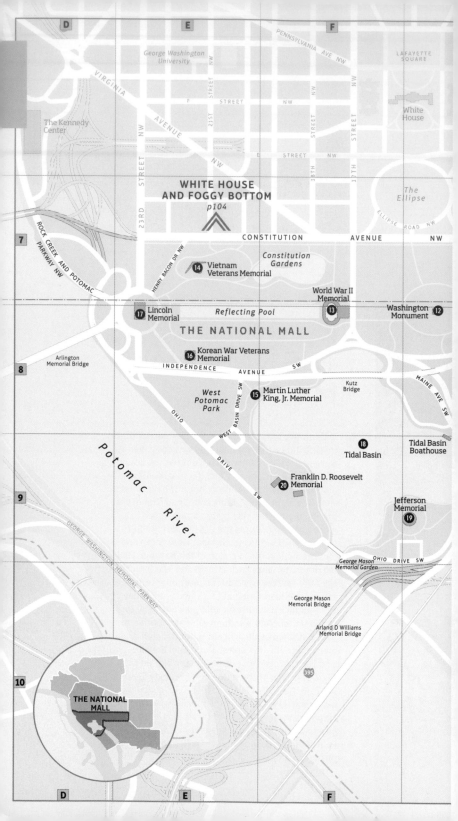

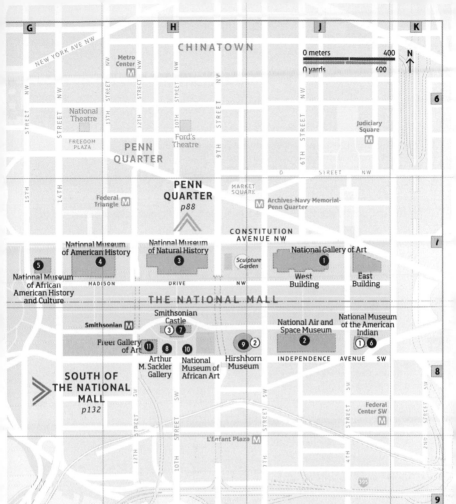

THE NATIONAL MALL

Must Sees

1. National Gallery of Art
2. National Air and Space Museum
3. National Museum of Natural History
4. National Museum of American History
5. National Museum of African American History and Culture

Experience More

6. National Museum of the American Indian
7. Smithsonian Castle
8. Arthur M. Sackler Gallery
9. Hirshhorn Museum
10. National Museum of African Art
11. Freer Gallery of Art

12. Washington Monument
13. World War II Memorial
14. Vietnam Veterans Memorial
15. Martin Luther King, Jr. Memorial
16. Korean War Veterans Memorial
17. Lincoln Memorial
18. Tidal Basin
19. Jefferson Memorial
20. Franklin D. Roosevelt Memorial

Eat

1. Mitsitam Café
2. Dolcezza Coffee & Gelato

NATIONAL GALLERY OF ART

◉ J7 **⌂ Between 3rd & 9th Sts & Constitution Ave, NW on the National Mall** **Ⓜ Archives-Navy Memorial-Penn Quarter, Judiciary Square, Smithsonian** **🚌 32, 34, 36, 70** **🕙 10am–5pm daily** **🔒 Jan 1, Dec 25** **🌐 nga.gov**

Housing one of the world's great collections of art, the National Gallery is itself an architectural masterpiece, and boasts a collection that includes over 150,000 paintings, prints, sculptures, and virtually every other type of artwork imaginable.

The gallery's two buildings are an unusual pair. The beautiful West Building is a majestic Neo-Classical structure designed by John Russell Pope. Opened in 1941, it displays the core of the museum's collection. The airy East Building, a radically angular counterpoint built by famed architect I. M. Pei in 1978, is a huge, fluid space, with galleries on either side holding works by modern and contemporary artists. Its lofty atrium is dominated by Alexander Calder's last and largest work, a huge mobile designed especially for the space. The open, green, and delightful Sculpture Garden lies next to the West Building.

ANDREW MELLON

In the 1920s, American financier and statesman Andrew Mellon began traveling the world and collecting art, including works from Russia's Hermitage. He offered his collection to the country in 1936, along with the funds to build a national gallery.

Did You Know?

Architect I. M. Pei designed the East Building in the shape of two triangles.

① The well-known biblical story of Daniel is depicted in the powerful *Daniel in the Lion's Den* by Peter Paul Rubens (c 1014–1016), one of the 17th century's greatest masters.

② Despite its light palette and tranquil atmosphere, Edward Hopper's 1939 *Ground Swell* reflects motifs of loneliness and escape that were typical of the artist's works.

③ A large, dramatic triangular atrium is the focus of the trapezoidal East Building, which was completed in 1978.

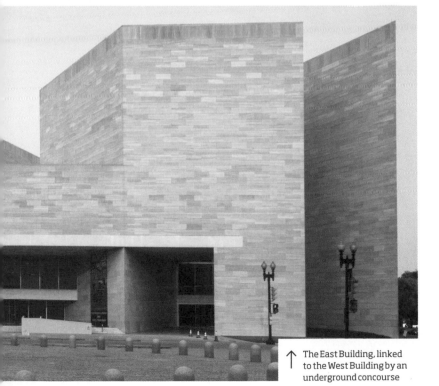

↑ The East Building, linked to the West Building by an underground concourse

Exploring the National Gallery of Art

The West Building holds the majority of the collection, with significant exhibits of Byzantine and Renaissance art, as well as a dazzling array of Impressionist works by Monet, Cassatt, and Renoir, among others. Pei's triangular East Building is home to modern and contemporary works. Renovations added 12,250 sq ft (1,138 sq m), making room for important works by Pablo Picasso, Mark Rothko, Alexander Calder, Barbara Kruger, and other artists. The Sculpture Garden features works by artists such as Calder, Marc Chagall, and Tony Smith.

↑ Works by Rothko in the National Gallery's modern art collections

Did You Know?

Alexander Calder's *Untitled* was the last sculpture he ever made.

Calder's mobile *Untitled* (1976), on display in the East Building atrium ↑

Top Collections

13th- to 16th-century Italian Art

▷ The collection features art that illustrates the transition from the Byzantine influence to the more expressive and realistic Renaissance style. Highlights include Pietro Perugino's *The Crucifixion with the Virgin, St. John, St. Jerome and St. Mary Magdalene*, Raphael's *The Alba Madonna* (1510), called by one writer "the supreme compositional achievement of Renaissance painting," and Fra Angelico and Fra Filippo Lippi's *Adoration of the Magi* (c 1440/1460) *(right)*.

16th-century Italian, Spanish, and French Art

The 1500s were the height of Italian Classicism. *Christ at the Sea of Galilee* (c 1575/1580) by Venetian master Jacopo Tintoretto typifies the style. The emotionally intense painting portrays Christ standing on the shore. There are also works by Titian and Raphael.

17th- to 18th-century Italian, Spanish, and French Art

Among these works is El Greco's *Christ Cleansing the Temple* (pre-1570), which demonstrates 16th-century Italian influence. El Greco ("The Greek") signed his real name, Domenikos Theotokopoulos, to the panel.

17th-century Dutch and Flemish Art

This collection holds a number of Old Masters including works by Van Dyck, Rubens, Vermeer, and Rembrandt. *Girl With a Red Hat* (c 1666) by Johannes Vermeer is a masterpiece demonstrating the artist's virtuosity in harmonizing light with brilliant color.

19th-century French Art

◁ One of the best Impressionist collections outside Paris, this includes Claude Monet's *The Bridge at Argenteuil* (1874) *(left)*. Post-Impressionist works include Toulouse-Lautrec's *Quadrille at the Moulin Rouge* (1892), depicting a dancer.

American Art

An important collection, this shows European influence, but in themes that are resolutely American. Examples include James McNeill Whistler's *Mother of Pearl and Silver: The Andalusian* (1888-1900) and *Breezing Up (A Fair Wind)* (1873-6), a masterpiece by the American Realist Winslow Homer.

Modern and Contemporary Art

The collection includes *Untitled* (1976), a vast mobile by Alexander Calder, Henry Moore's bronze sculpture *Knife Edge Mirror Two Piece* (1977-8), and works by Lichtenstein, Pollock, Rothko, and others.

Sculpture Garden

The elegant Sculpture Garden showcases 17 sculptures, including pieces by Louise Bourgeois and Joan Miró. Transformed into an ice rink in winter and a concert venue in summer, the garden functions both as an outdoor gallery and as a pleasant oasis within the city.

② Ⓜ Ⓨ ▣ ⚑

NATIONAL AIR AND SPACE MUSEUM

📍 J8 🏠 655 Jefferson Dr, SW Ⓜ Smithsonian 🚌 32, 34, 36, 52 🕐 10am–5:30pm daily (renovations ongoing, check website) 🌐 airandspace.si.edu

At its core, this museum celebrates one of the oldest human dreams: to break the bonds of earth, to fly, and reach for the stars. In its lofty, light-filled galleries, scores of famous planes hang overhead, while the floor is filled with rockets, spacecraft, and artifacts tracing the story of flight.

A great place for all enthusiasts of flight, the remarkable National Air and Space Museum attracts over seven million visitors every year. Reflecting the idea of flight, the soaring architecture of the 1976 building complements the thousands of exhibits on display within. The museum serves up a mind-bending array of sights and experiences, geared for all ages, that fire the imagination. Here visitors can learn about the origins of flight, admire some of the world's most storied air- and spacecraft, and discover the long road of innovation, failure, and success that led humans from wood and fabric wings to Mars landings.

GALLERY GUIDE

Both floors house themed displays. The first floor has a public observatory and a food court; the second has the Lockheed Martin IMAX® Theater and the Einstein Planetarium. Aircraft and spacecraft are suspended from the lofty ceilings.

↑ The red Lockheed Vega of Amelia Earhart, the first woman to make a solo transatlantic flight

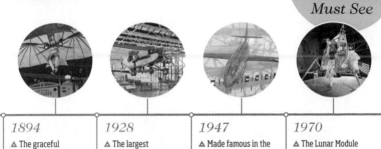

Timeline

1894
△ The graceful Lilienthal Glider developed by German aeronautical pioneer Otto Lilienthal lays the foundation for the Wright Brothers' flight experiments.

1928
△ The largest commercial plane in existence when introduced in 1926, the Ford Tri-Motor becomes known as "The Tin Goose."

1947
△ Made famous in the movie *The Right Stuff*, the Bell X-1 is the plane in which legendary pilot Chuck Yeager breaks the sound barrier in 1947.

1970
△ The Lunar Module LM-2 shuttles two astronauts from the Command Module orbiting the moon to the surface and back.

↑ The "America by Air" exhibit, outlining the history and global effect of the US airline industry

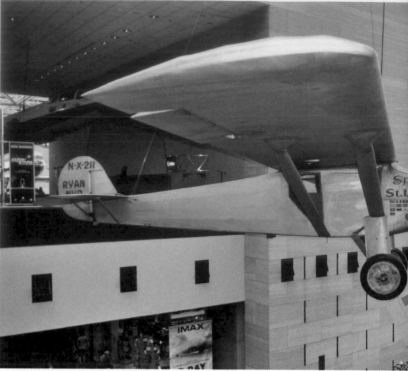

Exploring the National Air and Space Museum

There is a wealth of legendary planes and spacecraft here, like the *Wright Flyer* and the *Spirit of St. Louis*. But tucked away are also many lesser-known treats, like John Glenn's space suit and a Fokker T-2 that made the first nonstop US transcontinental flight in 1923. Exhibits such as "America by Air," "Space Race," and "Apollo to the Moon" highlight unique chapters in flight and space exploration, while interactive displays allow visitors to touch a real moon rock, walk through the Skylab space station, or use a flight simulator to fly a fighter jet.

↑ The *Spirit of St. Louis*, in which the 25-year-old Charles Lindbergh made the first solo transatlantic flight in May 1927

> 🔍 HIDDEN GEM
> ### Flight Simulators
>
> Flight simulators offer virtual reality, capsule, and traditional flight simulations. For a fee, these give visitors experiences that range from flying a World War I triplane to taking an exciting space walk.

←

The historic Mercury *Friendship 7* capsule, in which astronaut John Glenn became the first American to orbit the earth in 1961

INSIDER TIP
Tours for Trekkies

To celebrate the infinite diversity among its visitors, the museum - which says it is one of the galaxy's most popular attractions - offers an audio tour in Klingon via its smartphone app.

1 The soaring "Boeing Milestones of Flight" gallery highlights major firsts in aviation and space travel, including the groundbreaking SpaceShipOne.

2 One of the museum's most popular artifacts is the touchable moon rock in the "Boeing Milestones of Flight" exhibit.

3 Artifacts in the "Space Race" gallery, including John Glenn's space suit, trace the breakneck rivalry between the US and USSR from 1957 to 1975.

Geology, Gems & Minerals

Did You Know?

Overall this huge museum covers an area equivalent to the size of 18 football fields.

The rotunda's massive African bush elephant, one of the highlights of the museum ↑

3 Ⓜ️ 🖥 🏛

NATIONAL MUSEUM OF NATURAL HISTORY

📍 H7 🏛 Constitution Ave & 10th St, NW Ⓜ️ Smithsonian, Federal Triangle 🚌 32, 34, 36
🕐 10am–5:30pm daily 🚫 Dec 25 🌐 mnh.si.edu

Dedicated to inspiring curiosity and discovery about our natural world, from ancient life forms and our earliest ancestors to the diverse cultures of today, the National Museum of Natural History has plenty to fascinate all ages, making this one of the most popular museums on the National Mall, with seven million annual visitors.

The museum, which opened in 1910, preserves cultural and historical artifacts and collects samples of fossils and living creatures from land and sea. Visiting the museum is a vast undertaking, so sample the best of the exhibits and leave the rest for return visits. The expansive David H. Koch Hall of Fossils explores how the earth evolved from deep time to present. With its cutting edge exhibits and hands-on fossil specimens, it is popular with children, while the Ocean Hall delights young and old alike. The stunning Hall of Mammals has 274 specimens, and looks at how they adapted to changes in habitat and climate over millions of years.

↑ The museum's simple Neo-Classical exterior

↑ Marine specimens, high-definition videos, and the latest technology at the Sant Ocean Hall, allowing exploration of the ocean's past, present, and future

↑ The Hall of Mammals, filled with dramatic representations explaining the diversity of mammals

GALLERY GUIDE

The first floor's main exhibitions include dinosaur fossils, human origins, mammals, and marine life. Mummies are on the second level, alongside the Gems and Minerals collection, the Live Insect Zoo, and the Live Butterfly Pavilion. Q?rius, an interactive learning space on the ground and first floors, is popular with teenagers.

④ 🛈 🍴 🖶 🛍

NATIONAL MUSEUM OF AMERICAN HISTORY

📍G7 🚇Between 12th & 14th Sts, NW & Constitution Ave Ⓜ Smithsonian, Federal Triangle 🚌32, 34, 36 🕐10am–5:30pm daily 🚫Dec 25 🌐americanhistory.si.edu

This charming museum is filled with interesting artifacts from America's past. From a Colonial gunboat and Lincoln's hat to Kermit the Frog and Dorothy's ruby slippers, the objects cover unique moments and cultural touchstones in American history.

The museum has a flair for gathering its fascinating artifacts into powerful and informative exhibits. From the American Revolution to the space race, displays follow the nation's journey from its origins to its future. "America on the Move" tells the story of a mobile nation, while "Within These Walls" illustrates America's history through a real house that once stood in Massachusetts and the stories of five families that occupied it over 200 years. This is also a great museum for children, with lots of interactive displays, artifacts with wow-power, and instantly recognizable pieces like the Star-Spangled Banner and Mr. Rogers' red sweater.

Did You Know?
About 8 ft (2.5 m) of the Star-Spangled Banner is missing as over the years people took pieces as souvenirs.

GALLERY GUIDE

The first floor features science and transportation exhibits alongside Spark!Lab. The next floor has the Star-Spangled Banner and the groundbreaking exhibition, "Many Voices, One Nation", which explores the diversity of the American people and how they continue to shape the nation. The third floor offers the "First Ladies" exhibit and the gunboat *Philadelphia*.

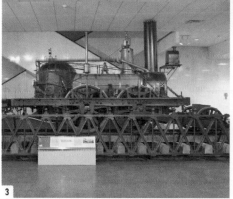

[1] SparkLab invites kids to participate in entertaining science experiments in a supervised environment.

[2] The rough, open wooden gunboat _Philadelphia_ was sunk in 1776 while defending Lake Champlain, whose cold waters preserved it until its recovery and restoration in 1935.

[3] The oldest operable locomotive in the world, the 1831 wood and steel _John Bull_, named for a fictional English gentleman, ran between New York City and Philadelphia.

↑ The Star-Spangled Banner, inspiration for the Francis Scott Key lyrics that became the US national anthem

5 💻 🎒

NATIONAL MUSEUM OF AFRICAN AMERICAN HISTORY AND CULTURE

📍 G7 🏛 1400 Constitution Ave, NW Ⓜ Smithsonian 🚌 13, 52 🕐 10am–5:30pm daily 🚫 Dec 25 🌐 nmaahc.si.edu

This powerful museum traces African American history from the roots of slavery to the election of an African American president and beyond. The galleries begin 70 ft (21 m) underground with exhibits on slavery and segregation, rising to higher, brighter floors that focus on emancipation and civil rights, and offer an inspirational look at a people striving to take their rightful place in the nation.

The museum's collections are designed to support three pillars of the African American story: History, Culture, and Community. These are told through ten major exhibit galleries. In addition to slavery and segregation, these halls highlight African American contributions to sports, music, visual arts, and military history. "Hometown Hub" examines ten geographical centers of unique African American experience, such as Chicago and South Carolina. The museum also houses a 350-seat theater and the award-winning Sweet Home Café. The museum is so popular that timed-entry passes are often needed. Advance passes are available online. During off-peak times, when visitation is lower, visitors can enter the museum on weekdays without passes.

100,000

The estimated number of people who escaped slavery through the Underground Railroad.

① *Musical Crossroads* tells the story of African American music from the arrival of the first Africans to the present.

② The Serenity Room is a space to meditate on the thought-provoking themes and exhibits.

③ The striking building is covered in 3,600 bronze-colored cast-aluminum panels that form a lattice, symbolizing upward striving.

Exhibit depicting the ↑
1968 Olympics Black
Power salute by Tommie
Smith and John Carlos

Timeline

Before 1864
△ The Underground
Railroad leads people
to freedom, and Harriet
Tubman (1822-1913)
is one of its most suc-
cessful "conductors."

1876–1968
△ Defying the prevailing
segregation laws, four
African Americans
occupy these stools at a
Woolworths store on
February 1, 1960.

1955–1968
△ America's Civil
Rights movement
effectively ends seg-
regation and improves
the lives of millions of
African Americans.

2013
△ American activists
Patrisse Cullors,
Alicia Garza, and
Opal Tometi form
the Black Lives
Matter Network.

EXPERIENCE MORE

6 Ⓜ 🖥 🏛

National Museum of the American Indian

📍J8 🏛 The National Mall, 4th St & Independence Ave, SW Ⓜ L'Enfant Plaza 🕐 10am–5:30pm daily 🌐 americanindian.si.edu

Anyone who has ever been fascinated by the history or culture of Native Americans will want to visit this elegant museum. With its sweeping natural curves reminiscent of the red-rock country of the American Southwest, the building is set in a landscape meant to reflect the Native American connection to the land.

Established in collaboration with the Native American communities throughout the western hemisphere, this is the only national museum dedicated to Indigenous peoples. The exhibits showcase the spiritual and daily lives of diverse peoples and encourage visitors to look beyond stereotypes. "Many Hands, Many Voices" features more than 3,500 objects, including beaded objects and artwork, and is a good place to start. Even more impressive are the exhibits that offer a first-hand look into the life and beliefs of numerous indigenous cultures. In "Nation to Nation," Native Americans tell their own stories and histories via artifacts and videos, focusing on both the destruction of their culture and on their resilience. In "Return to a Native Place" the focus is on the Algonquian peoples (the Nanticoke, Powhatan, and Piscataway) of the Chesapeake Bay region.

JAMES SMITHSON

Although he never visited the United States, English philanthropist James Smithson (1765–1829) left his fortune to "found at Washington [...] an establishment for the increase and diffusion of knowledge among men." Congress used his bequest to set up a foundation to administer all national museums, and the first Smithson collection was shown at the Smithsonian Castle in 1855.

JAMES SMITHSON

7 Ⓜ 🖥 🏛

Smithsonian Castle

📍H8 🏛 1000 Jefferson Dr, SW Ⓜ Smithsonian 🕐 8:30am–5:30pm daily 🌐 si.edu

Constructed of red sandstone in 1855, the ornate Victorian Smithsonian Castle served as the first home of the Smithsonian Institution, and today houses its information center and administrative offices. The South Tower Room was the first children's room in a Washington, DC

museum. Outside the castle is the rose garden, filled with beautiful hybrid tea roses.

Arthur M. Sackler Gallery

📍H8 🏛1050 Independence Ave, SW 🚇Smithsonian 🕐10am-5:30pm daily 🌐asia.si.edu

Dr. Arthur M. Sackler, a New York physician, started collecting Asian art in the 1950s. In 1982, he donated more than 1,000 artifacts, along with $4 million in funds, to the Smithsonian Institution to establish this museum.

Sackler's 3,000-piece collection is particularly rich in Chinese works, and highlights

> **INSIDER TIP**
> **Smithsonian Carousel**
>
> Kids and adults love the 1947 carousel set near the Smithsonian Castle. As well as its traditional music and ornately carved horses, there's also a popular sea dragon to ride.

↑ One of the pair of bronze *Lions of Timna* at the Sackler Gallery

include a stunning display of Chinese bronzes and jades, some dating back to 4000 BC. There are also 17th-century Ming ceramics and an extensive range of sculpture from India and Southeast Asia.

In 1987 the gallery acquired the impressive Vever Collection, which includes Islamic books from the 11th to the 19th centuries; 19th- and 20th-century Japanese prints; Japanese, Chinese, and Indian paintings; and modern photography.

Hirshhorn Museum

📍H8 🏛Independence Ave & 7th St, SW 🚇L'Enfant Plaza 🕐Museum: 10am-5:30pm daily; sculpture garden: 7:30am-dusk 🌐hirshhorn.si.edu

The Hirshhorn's building has been variously described as a doughnut or a flying saucer, but it is actually a four-story, not-quite-symmetrical cylinder. It is home to one of the greatest collections of modern art in the United States.

The museum's benefactor, Joseph H. Hirshhorn, was an eccentric, flamboyant Latvian immigrant who amassed

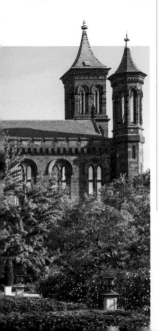

←

The Smithsonian Castle, built in imposing Gothic Revival style

6,000 pieces of contemporary art; the collection now has double that number. The main floor displays newly acquired work, while the second floor hosts temporary exhibitions. The third floor houses the permanent collection, which includes works by artists such as Alexander Calder, Arshile Gorky, Willem de Kooning, and John Singer Sargent. The sculpture garden outside includes pieces by Calder, Rodin, and Matisse.

National Museum of African Art

📍H8 🏛950 Independence Ave, SW 🚇Smithsonian 🕐10am-5:30pm daily 🌐africa.si.edu

This is the first US museum to concentrate solely on the art and culture of the African continent. The underground galleries are accessed through an entrance pavilion in the Enid A. Haupt Garden, in front of the Smithsonian Castle.

Visitors can explore three subterranean floors that hold the museum's 12,000-piece permanent collection, which includes both modern and ancient art from Africa. Traditional art in gold, bronze, and ceramic is on display, along with an extensive collection of masks. There is also a display of brightly colored, patterned *kente* cloth from Ghana, often used for special occasions and as a symbol of African nationalism. The Eliot Elisofon Photographic Archives (Eliot Elisofon was a famous photographer for *Life* magazine) contain over 550,000 prints and 120,000 ft (36,576 m) of film footage on African art and culture.

The museum hosts dance, music, and spoken-word events. There is also a full calendar of educational tours, lectures, and workshops, including many for children.

⑪ 👜 Freer Gallery of Art

📍H8 🚪Jefferson Dr & 12th St, SW Ⓜ Smithsonian 🕐10am–5:30pm daily 🌐asia.si.edu

Named after Charles Lang Freer, a railroad magnate who donated his collection of 9,000 pieces of American and Asian art to the Smithsonian, the Freer Gallery opened in 1923, becoming the first Smithsonian museum of art. Constructed in the Italian Renaissance style, the Freer has an attractive courtyard with a fountain. There are 19 galleries, most with skylights that illuminate a superb collection of Asian and American art. In the Asian Art collection are examples of Chinese, Japanese, and Korean art, including sculpture, ceramics, paintings, and folding screens. It also has a fine selection of Buddhist sculpture, as well as paintings and calligraphy from India.

There is also a select collection of American art.

The imposing granite pillars of Washington, DC's national World War II Memorial ↑

The most astonishing work is James McNeill Whistler's "The Peacock Room." Whistler painted a dining room for British shipowner Frederick Leyland in London, who found that it was not to his taste. Freer purchased the room in 1904 and had it dismantled and moved to Washington, DC. In contrast to the subtle elegance of the other rooms in the gallery, this one is a riot of blues, greens, and golds, with Whistler's gorgeously painted peacocks covering the walls and ceiling.

⑫ 🚫 👜 Washington Monument

📍G8 🚪Independence Ave at 17th St, SW Ⓜ Smithsonian 🕐9am–5pm daily (Memorial Day–Labor Day: to 10pm) 🌐nps.gov/wamo

Made from 36,000 pieces of marble and granite, this 555 ft (170 m) column is one of the city's most recognizable sights. Funds initially came from individual citizens, and building began in 1848. The Civil War and a shortage of funds stopped the work for 25 years. Then, in 1876, President Ulysses S. Grant authorized its completion. A slight change in the color of stone shows where construction resumed.

⑬ World War II Memorial

📍F8 🚪17th St, NW between Constitution & Independence Aves Ⓜ Smithsonian, Federal Triangle 🕐24 hrs daily 🌐nps.gov/nwwm

Sixteen million Americans served in World War II, and

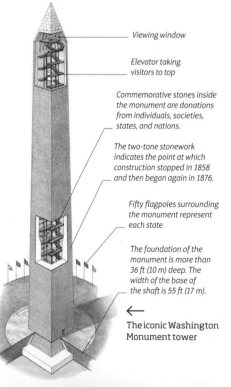

Viewing window

Elevator taking visitors to top

Commemorative stones inside the monument are donations from individuals, societies, states, and nations.

The two-tone stonework indicates the point at which construction stopped in 1858 and then began again in 1876.

Fifty flagpoles surrounding the monument represent each state

The foundation of the monument is more than 36 ft (10 m) deep. The width of the base of the shaft is 55 ft (17 m).

← The iconic Washington Monument tower

of those, 400,000 died. The 4,000 gold stars – the Field of Stars –on the Freedom Wall commemorate these war dead. Millions more ordinary citizens contributed to the war effort. The World War II Memorial honors their service and sacrifice. Its dedication ceremony on May 29, 2004, attracted 150,000 people, many of them veterans. The monument features a 43-ft- (13-m-) long pavilion on each side of the Rainbow Pool to represent the Atlantic and Pacific theaters of war. A granite pillar stands for each of the country's 56 states and territories during that time. Bas-relief panels by sculptor Ray Kaskey line both sides of the 17th Street entrance. They depict the many contributions that Americans made to the war effort: from enlistment and embarkation to medics in the field and Rosie the Riveter

(symbolizing the work done by American women).

Words spoken by generals and presidents are inscribed throughout the memorial, including these by General Douglas MacArthur marking the war's end: "Today the guns are silent… The skies no longer rain death – the seas bear only commerce – men everywhere walk upright in the sunlight. The entire world is quietly at peace."

🕙

Vietnam Veterans Memorial

📍E7 🏛22nd St & Constitution Ave, NW Ⓜ Smithsonian ⏱24 hrs daily 🌐nps.gov/vive

Maya Lin, a 21-year-old student at Yale University, submitted a design for the proposed Vietnam Veterans Memorial as part of her architecture course. One of 1,421 entries, Maya Lin's design was simple – two triangular black walls sinking into the earth at an angle of 125 degrees, one end pointing to the Lincoln Memorial, the other to the Washington Monument. On the walls would be inscribed the names, in chronological order, of the more than 58,000 Americans who died in the Vietnam War,

from the first death in 1959 to the last in 1975. Since the names are not in alphabetical order, there is a book listing all the names that correspond to a panel.

Lin received only a B grade in her college course, but she won the competition to design the memorial. It has become one of the most moving monuments on the National Mall. Veterans and their families leave tokens of remembrance – soft toys, poems, pictures, and bunches of flowers – at the site of their fallen soldier's name.

Nearby, an evocative statue of three soldiers awaiting airlift, sculpted by Frederick Hart, was added in 1984, and the Vietnam Women's Memorial was built in 1993.

EAT

Mitsitam Café
The National Museum of the American Indian (p80) houses this laid-back café, which offers traditional dishes of the Indigenous peoples of North and South America.

📍J8 🏛4th St & Independence Ave, SW 🌐americanindian si.edu

$$$

Dolcezza Coffee & Gelato
This café in the Hirshhorn Museum (p81) serves handmade ice creams and gourmet pastries along with espressos and teas.

📍H8 🏛Independence Ave & 7th St, SW 🌐hirshhorn. si.edu

$$$

 INSIDER TIP
Find Kilroy!

At the World War II Memorial, kids can have a great time hunting for the two iconic "Kilroy Was Here" images that are carved into the stone, similar to the ones that American GIs drew everywhere during the war.

The striking figures of the Korean War Veterans Memorial ↑

15

Martin Luther King, Jr. Memorial

📍F8 🏛1850 West Basin Dr, SW Ⓜ Smithsonian, Foggy Bottom-GWU 🕐24 hrs daily 🌐nps.gov/mlkm

Set among the famous cherry blossom trees of the Tidal Basin is the National Mall's first memorial to an African American. Dedicated on August 26, 2011, it commemorates the life and work of Dr. King. Designed by Chinese sculptor Lei Yixin, the memorial consists of two huge stone tablets – one features excerpts from King's speeches, while the other shows his figure emerging from the stone. The choice of a non-American sculptor proved highly controversial, as did King's stern expression.

16

Korean War Veterans Memorial

📍E8 🏛10 Daniel French Dr, SW Ⓜ Smithsonian, Foggy Bottom-GWU 🕐24 hrs daily 🌐nps.gov/kwvm

This memorial is a controversial tribute to a controversial war. Although 1.5 million Americans served in the conflict, war was never officially declared and it is known as "The Forgotten War."

Intense debate preceded the selection of the memorial's design. The Korean War Veterans Memorial was dedicated on July 27, 1995, on the 42nd anniversary of the armistice that ended the war. Nineteen larger-than-life stainless steel statues, a squad on patrol, are shown moving toward the American flag as their symbolic objective. On the south side is a polished black granite wall etched with the images of more than 2,400 veterans.

An inscription above the Pool of Remembrance reads: "Our nation honors her sons and daughters who answered the call to defend a country they never knew and a people they never met."

17 🏛

Lincoln Memorial

📍E8 🏛Constitution Ave between French & Bacon Dr Ⓜ Smithsonian, Foggy Bottom-GWU, then 20-min walk 🕐24 hrs daily 🌐nps. gov/linc

One of the least promising proposals for a memorial to President Lincoln was for a monument on swampy land to the west of the Washington Monument. Yet this was to become one of the city's most awe-inspiring sights. Looming over the Reflecting Pool is the

> **The Korean War Veterans Memorial was dedicated on July 27, 1995, on the 42nd anniversary of the armistice that ended the war.**

huge seated figure of Lincoln in his Neo-Classical "temple" with 36 Doric columns, one for each state at the time of his death. Today, it is a national touchstone for socially progressive movements. It is an icon of the Civil Rights movement, and it was from its steps in 1963 that Dr. King gave his "I Have a Dream" speech. Inside, engraved on the south wall is the Gettysburg Address *(p186)*. Above it is Jules Guerin's mural of the angel of truth freeing an enslaved person. Under the memorial there is a small area with exhibits about President Lincoln and a gift shop.

18

Tidal Basin

📍F9 🏛Boathouse: 1501 Maine Ave, SW Ⓜ Smithsonian

The Tidal Basin was built in 1897 to catch the Potomac's overflow and prevent flooding. In 1912, cherry trees, a gift of the Japanese government, were planted along the shores of the man-made lake. During the two weeks when they bloom (mid-March to mid-April) the area teems with visitors who come to walk under canopies of gracefully arching branches laden with pink blossoms, picnic on the lawns, or go paddleboating in the Tidal Basin.

Ⓜ Ⓗ

Jefferson Memorial

📍 G9 🏛 South bank of the Tidal Basin Ⓜ Smithsonian 🕐 24 hrs daily 🌐 nps.gov/thje

Thomas Jefferson (p188) was a political philosopher, architect, musician, book collector, horticulturist, diplomat, inventor, scientist, and the third president of the US, from 1801 to 1809. He played a significant part in drafting the Declaration of Independence yet was a life-long slave owner who also proposed the idea of the removal of Indigenous peoples east of the Mississippi. Designed by John Russell Pope, this Neo Classical memorial was dedicated in 1943 and holds a 19-ft- (6-m-) tall bronze of Jefferson.

> ### HISTORY OF THE NATIONAL MALL
>
> In 1789, Frenchman Pierre L'Enfant (1754–1825), the city's first town planner, envisioned a grand avenue running west from the Capitol, but years later the area remained undeveloped. It wasn't until the end of the Civil War, in 1865, that Lincoln ordered work to begin again, and the National Mall began to take on its park-like appearance. The addition of museums and memorials in the 20th century confirmed the National Mall as Washington, DC's cultural heart and "America's Front Yard."

The memorial also has a bookstore, a gift shop, and a small museum.

Ⓗ

Franklin D. Roosevelt Memorial

📍 F9 🏛 400 W Basin Dr, SW Ⓜ Smithsonian, then 25-min walk 🕐 24 hrs daily 🌐 nps.gov/fdrm

Franklin D. Roosevelt once told Supreme Court Justice Felix Frankfurter, "If they are to put up any memorial to me… I should like it to consist of a block about the size of this," pointing to his desk.

It took more than 50 years for a fitting monument to be built, but Roosevelt's plea for modesty was not heeded

Opened in 1997, this memorial is a huge park of four granite open-air rooms, one for each of Roosevelt's terms. The first room has a bronze bas-relief. In the second room, *Breadline* by George Segal recalls the Great Depression, during which Roosevelt was reelected three times. Neil Estern's sculpture in the third room portrays the president, a polio survivor, sitting in a wheelchair hidden by his Navy cape, with his beloved little terrier Fala by his side. In the last room, waterfalls cascade down into a series of pools, whose waters reflect the peace that Roosevelt was so keen to achieve before his death.

↓ The memorial dedicated to Franklin D. Roosevelt

A relief of Roosevelt's funeral cortège was carved into the granite wall by artist Leonard Baskin.

Third room

Sculpture by George Segal

The Visitor Center, where the wheelchair used by FDR after he had polio is displayed.

Second room

FDR initiated the New Deal in the 1930s to create jobs and provide immediate relief during the Great Depression.

The fourth room honors FDR's life and legacy. A statue of his wife Eleanor stands here.

Dramatic waterfalls

Statue by Neil Estern

Bas-relief of FDR's inaugural parade

A SHORT WALK
THE NATIONAL MALL

Distance 1.5 miles (2.5 km) **Nearest Metro** Smithsonian
Time 30 minutes

This 1 mile (1.5 km) boulevard between the Capitol and the Washington Monument is the city's cultural heart, with the many different museums of the Smithsonian Institution set along this green strip. At the northeast corner of the National Mall is the National Gallery of Art and its Sculpture Garden. Standing directly opposite the gallery is one of the most popular museums in the world – the National Air and Space Museum, a vast, soaring construction of steel and glass. Both the National Museum of American History and the National Museum of Natural History, on the north side of the National Mall, draw huge numbers of visitors.

The **Smithsonian Castle** (p80), *once home to the initial collections of the numerous museums along the National Mall and today the main information center of the Smithsonian Institution*

The **National Museum of Natural History** (p74), *designed in Neo-Classical style and opened to the public in 1910*

The **National Museum of American History** (p76), *documenting every aspect of US history, from George Washington's uniform to Lincoln's top hat*

9TH STREET NW

MADISON DRIVE NW

START

The **Freer Gallery of Art** (p82), *with a trove of Asian art in addition to a superb Whistler collection*

FINISH

JEFFERSON DRIVE SW

The **Arthur M. Sackler Gallery** (p81), *an extensive collection of Asian art donated to the nation by New Yorker Arthur Sackler*

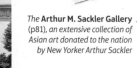

The pleasant courtyard at the Freer Gallery

The **National Museum of African Art** (p81), *founded in 1965 with a comprehensive collection of ancient and modern African art*

Did You Know?

In 1881, its opening year, the Arts and Industries Building hosted President Garfield's inaugural ball.

The superb **National Gallery of Art** (p66), with paintings and other works of art that chronicle the history of art from the Middle Ages to the 20th century

National Gallery of Art, West Building

Locator Map
For more detail see p64

THE NATIONAL MALL

National Gallery of Art, Sculpture Garden

CONSTITUTION AVENUE NW

7TH STREET NW

MADISON DRIVE NW

7TH STREET NW

National Gallery of Art, East Building

The **National Air and Space Museum** (p70), with its clean, modern design echoing the technological advances in aviation illustrated by the spectacular exhibits inside

INDEPENDENCE AVENUE SW

0 meters   100
0 yards   100

N ↑

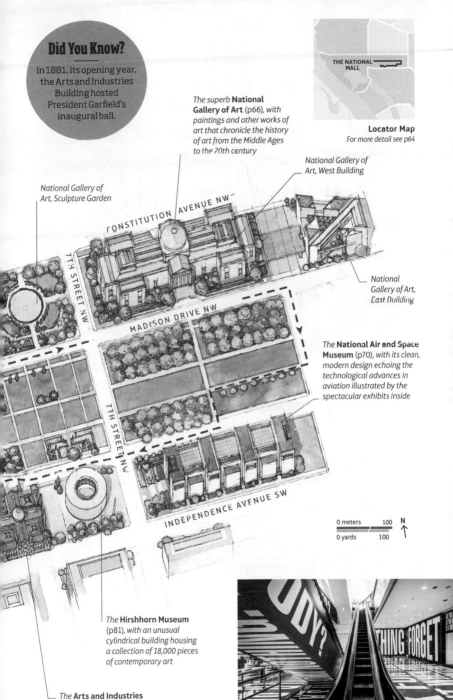

The **Hirshhorn Museum** (p81), with an unusual cylindrical building housing a collection of 18,000 pieces of contemporary art

The **Arts and Industries Building**, a masterpiece of Victorian architecture originally built to contain exhibits from the 1876 Centennial Exposition in Philadelphia

↑ Barbara Kruger's *Belief+Doubt* installation at the Hirshhorn

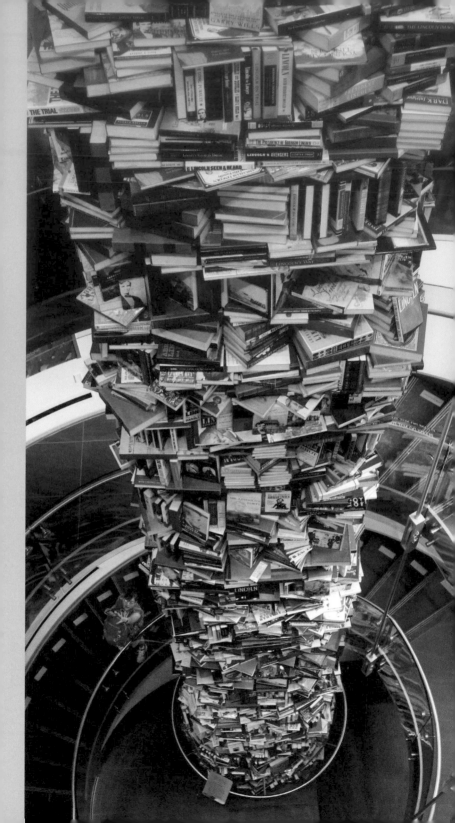

PENN QUARTER

Bordered by the Capitol to the east and the White House to the west, Washington, DC's Penn Quarter was the heart of the city at the start of the 20th century. F Street, the city's first paved road, bustled with shops, bars, newspaper offices, and churches, as well as horses and carriages. Penn Quarter was also an important residential neighborhood. The upper classes kept elegant homes, while middle-class merchants lived above their shops. By the 1950s suburbia had lured people away, and in the 1980s Penn Quarter was a mixture of boarded-up buildings and discount shops. The 1990s saw a dramatic change and the beginnings of regeneration, as the Capital One Arena attracted trendy eateries and upscale brands. Today, the area has some fantastic dining, shopping, and entertainment options, and with the addition of CityCenterDC in 2015, it continues to flourish as a thriving hub of activity.

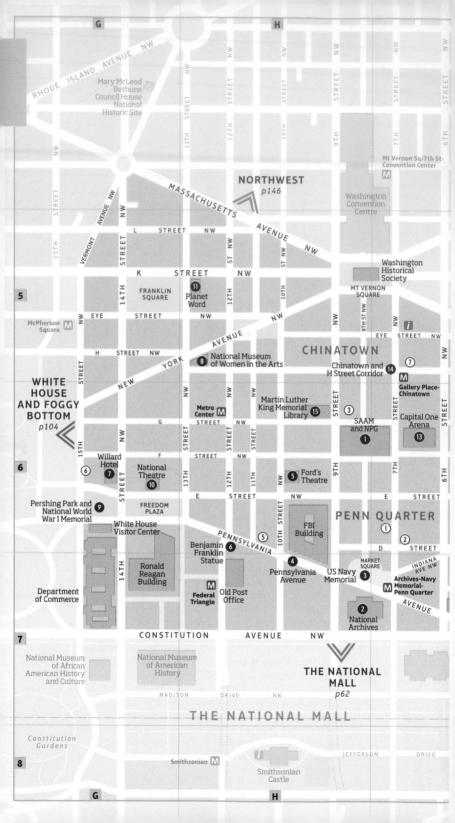

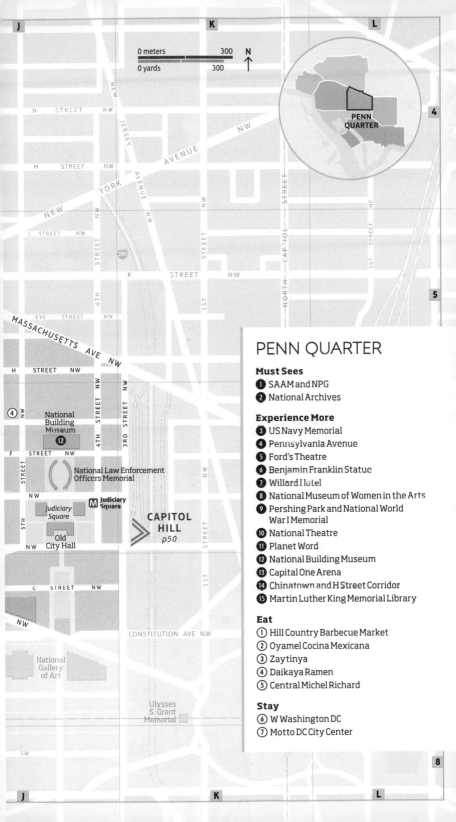

PENN QUARTER

Must Sees
1 SAAM and NPG
2 National Archives

Experience More
3 US Navy Memorial
4 Pennsylvania Avenue
5 Ford's Theatre
6 Benjamin Franklin Statue
7 Willard Hotel
8 National Museum of Women in the Arts
9 Pershing Park and National World War I Memorial
10 National Theatre
11 Planet Word
12 National Building Museum
13 Capital One Arena
14 Chinatown and H Street Corridor
15 Martin Luther King Memorial Library

Eat
1 Hill Country Barbecue Market
2 Oyamel Cocina Mexicana
3 Zaytinya
4 Daikaya Ramen
5 Central Michel Richard

Stay
6 W Washington DC
7 Motto DC City Center

CAPITOL HILL p50

SAAM AND NPG

📍H6 🏛8th & F Sts, NW Ⓜ Gallery Place-Chinatown
🕐11:30am–7pm daily 🌐americanart.si.edu, npg.si.edu

EXPERIENCE Penn Quarter

Two exceptional museums, the Smithsonian American Art Museum (SAAM) and the National Portrait Gallery (NPG), share one of the city's most iconic buildings, linked by a courtyard with a striking Norman Foster roof. The Greek Revival-style National Historic Landmark, once the Patent Office, was bought by the Smithsonian in 1958.

In 1829, John Varden set out to display his private art trove, eventually finding space in the Patent Office Building – the museum's present home – making him the de facto curator for government-owned treasures. From 1858 to 1906 his collection was merged with the newly formed Smithsonian National Gallery of Art. By 1968, the Smithsonian had not only saved the elegant Patent Office Building from demolition, they moved the collection back home as well. Today, SAAM houses one of the world's largest collections of American art, revealing the country's artistic and cultural history from the colonial era to present times.

The National Portrait Gallery, founded by Congress in 1962, shares the landmark space, displaying portraits of those who have made significant contributions to the history, development, and culture of the United States.

↑ Dr. Michael DeBakey's bust at the National Portrait Gallery

The spectacular, modern ↑
Kogod Courtyard linking
the twin museums

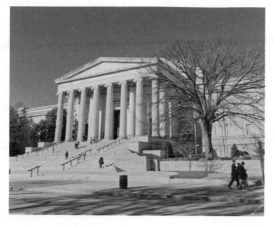

Beautiful facade of the National Portrait Gallery in the United States capital

→

NPG's ornate Great Hall, with its vaulted ceiling and intricate flooring

OLD PATENT MODEL MUSEUM

Often called the "Temple of Invention," this extraordinary Greek Revival landmark was once teeming with small machines and contraptions. The building was designed to showcase the working models that inventors submitted alongside their patent applications and was once a very popular tourist attraction.

The chic Lincoln Gallery at the SAAM that exhibits contemporary artworks ↑

EXPLORING THE SAAM

The museum houses one of the world's largest collections of American art, illuminating the country's artistic and cultural history from the Colonial era to today. It is a matchless record of the American experience, capturing the identity, spirit, and dreams of people over the centuries. The SAAM holds significant aspects of visual culture, including works by folk and Latin American artists, as well as more than 2,000 pieces by African American artists. The collections chart the nation's growth from a young republic with landscapes such as Thomas Moran's Westerns, through the 20th-century realism via Andrew Wyeth and the Modernist Georgia O'Keeffe. It also has important contemporary art, American Impressionist paintings, and masterpieces from the Gilded Age, as well as the country's largest trove of New Deal art. More than 7,000 artists are represented

↑ Mary Cassatt's 1902 painting The Caress, at the SAAM

here. Among the highlights are 19th-century works by Winslow Homer; self-taught art by James Hampton; Impressionist art by Mary Cassatt; contemporary works by Christo and Roy Lichtenstein, including his 6.5-ton (5,900-kg) sculpture *Modern Head* (1989), which greets visitors at the main entrance, and the mammoth, 51-channel video installation titled *Electronic Superhighway: Continental U.S., Alaska, Hawaii* (1995) by Korean American artist Nam June Paik.

> **The museum is a matchless record of the American experience, capturing the identity, spirit, and dreams of people over the centuries.**

←

The Thundershower (c 1917-18) by H. Lyman Saÿen, a mix of European Modernism and Native American patterns

EXPLORING THE NPG

The NPG is America's family album, magnificently combining history, biography, and art in its collections. By highlighting those who have made significant contributions to the history, development, and culture of the people of the United States, the gallery keeps generations of remarkable Americans in the company of their fellow citizens. There are presidents and religious figures, visionaries and villains, artists and activists – all individuals who have shaped America's national identity. The portraits are fascinating because they reveal their subjects and illustrate the times in which they were produced. There are over 23,000 images in the permanent collection, which includes a variety of media, from paintings, photographs, and sculptures to digital works and time-based media.

Figures such as Michelle Obama, Rosa Parks, Dr. Martin Luther King, Jr., Babe Ruth, Casey Stengel, Tallulah Bankhead, and Judy Garland, are portrayed in a range of media, including oils, clay, and bronze. In 1857, Congress

↑ Amy Sherald's evocative 2018 portrait *First Lady Michelle Obama*

commissioned George Peter Alexander Healy to paint portraits of the presidents. The chronologically ordered depictions of all of the US's leaders remains the heart of the gallery's exhibitions.

Located on the second floor, Nelson Shanks's 7-ft- (2-m-) high group portrait The Four Justices is a tribute to the US Supreme's four female justices. On the third floor, visitors will find the Great Hall with its kaleidoscopic vaulted ceiling of tiles and medallions. A frieze showing the evolution of technology in America also runs around the room.

TOP 5 PORTRAITS AT NPG

Lansdowne Portrait (1796)
Painted from life, Gilbert Stuart depicts George Washington as fierce and guarded, a far cry from his public persona.

Abraham Lincoln (1865)
Alexander Gardner's "cracked-plate" portrait has only one copy, which was captured only two months before the president's assassination.

Billie Holiday (1959)
Herman Leonard's hauntingly evocative selenium-toned gelatin silver print depicts the jazz legend crooning into a microphone.

Barack Obama (2018)
A striking, floral portrait of the 44th president, by one of the US's most dynamic contemporary artists, Kehinde Wiley.

Bill and Melinda Gates (2010)
Oil and collage of tech super giants turned global philanthropists by Jon R. Friedman.

↑ Portaits of 20th-century American figures on display at the National Portrait Gallery

The Rotunda of Rights, with argon-filled cases holding the three Charters of Freedom ↑

2 🅜 🍽 🛍

NATIONAL ARCHIVES

📍H7 🏛Constitution Ave between 7th & 9th Sts, NW Ⓜ Archives-Navy Memorial-Penn Quarter 🕐10am–5:30pm daily 🚫Thanksgiving, Dec 25 🌐archives.gov

In the 1930s, Congress recognized the need to preserve the country's paper records before they deteriorated or were lost or destroyed. The result was the National Archives, opened in 1934, which house the US's most important historical and legal documents. These include the Constitution, the Declaration of Independence, and the Bill of Rights, as well as a 1297 copy of the Magna Carta.

> 💬 INSIDER TIP
> **Beat the Lines**
>
> If you plan to visit the archives during high season (April–July), beat the lines by reserving timed-entry tickets ($1.50 each online). Allow about 30 minutes for the Charters of Freedom, but another one or two hours for the rest of the exhibits, especially "Public Vaults."

Also here are millions of documents, photographs, films, and sound recordings going back over two centuries. A permanent exhibition, "Public Vaults," contains interactive displays and about 1,100 documents and artifacts, ranging from George Washington's letters and Abraham Lincoln's wartime telegrams to a recording of a speech by Theodore Roosevelt. The exhibit has five individual themes, including "We the People," with documents on family and citizenship, and "To Form a More Perfect Union," which displays records of Liberty and Law.

→

One of two 1936 murals by Barry Faulkner with fictional representations of the Declaration of Independence and US Constitution

EXPERIENCE MORE

250,000

filing cabinets can be filled with the documents housed in the National Archives.

THE CONSTITUTION

Delegates from the 13 original American states met in 1787 in Philadelphia. Months of debate followed as they drafted the framework for a new country. Cooperation and compromise finally led to the creation of the Constitution, which outlines the powers of the central government and the makeup of Congress. The majority of states ratified the document, giving up some of their power "in order to form a more perfect union."

❸
US Navy Memorial

🔲 H7 🏛 Market Sq, Pennsylvania Ave between 7th & 9th Sts, NW Ⓜ Archives-Navy Memorial-Penn Quarter

The memorial centers on the statue of a single sailor standing on a vast map of the world. Sculpted in bronze by Stanley Bleifeld in 1990, it is a poignant tribute to the men and women who have served in the US Navy. Behind the memorial, the **Naval Heritage Center** has historical exhibits and portraits of famous naval personnel. A free film, *At Sea*, is shown at 2pm.

Naval Heritage Center

🏛 🔲 701 Pennsylvania Ave, NW 🕘 9:30am–5pm daily 🚫 Jan 1, Thanksgiving, Dec 25 🌐 navymemorial.org

❹
Pennsylvania Avenue

🔲 H7 🏛 Pennsylvania Ave Ⓜ Federal Triangle, Archives-Navy Memorial-Penn Quarter

When the original architect of Washington, DC, Pierre L'Enfant, drew up his plans in 1789 for the capital of the new United States, he imagined a grand boulevard running through the center of the city, from the presidential palace to the legislative building. For the first 200 years of its history, however, Pennsylvania Avenue fell sadly short of his dreams. In the early 19th century it was simply a muddy footpath through the woods. Paved in 1833, it became part of a neighborhood of boarding houses, shops, and hotels. During the Civil War, the street deteriorated into an area of saloons and gambling dens.

When President Kennedy's inaugural parade proceeded down the avenue in 1961, he said, "It's a disgrace – fix it." Congress was spurred to set up a plan to revitalize the area. Today, the avenue is a clean, tree-lined street with parks, memorials, theaters, shops, hotels, museums, and government buildings – a suitably grand setting for all inaugural parades.

↑ The US Capitol at the end of Pennsylvania Avenue

PRESIDENTIAL INAUGURAL PARADES

The tradition of inaugural parades to mark a new president taking office started in 1809, when the military accompanied President James Madison from his Virginia home to Washington, DC. The first parade to include floats was held in 1841 for President William Henry Harrison. In 1985, freezing weather forced Ronald Reagan's inaugural ceremony indoors to the Capitol Rotunda. A record crowd of approximately 1.8 million attended the 2009 parade for Barack Obama. In 2021, the inauguration of Joe Biden was a more subdued affair due to COVID-19 restrictions, with a "Field of Flags" replacing the usual crowds.

5 ⚡ Ⓜ 🛍️

Ford's Theatre

📍H6 🏠511 10th St between E & F Sts, NW Ⓜ Gallery Place-Chinatown, Metro Center 🕐9am–4:30pm daily with timed pass (except matinee or rehearsal days - book online) 🌐fords.org

John T. Ford, a theatrical producer, built this small jewel of a theater in 1863. Washington, DC was a Civil War boomtown, and the theater enjoyed great popularity. Its fate was sealed, however, on April 14, 1865, when President Abraham Lincoln was shot here by John Wilkes Booth while watching a performance. After the tragedy, people stopped patronizing the theater, and Ford was forced to sell the building. It was left to spiral into decay for nearly a century until the government decided to restore it to its original splendor. Today, the theater stages small productions and offers tours of the building, which looks much as it did in 1865. Across the street, visitors can tour **Petersen House**, where Lincoln died the next morning.

Petersen House

🕐9:30am–5:30pm daily with free timed ticket

Did You Know?

Despite only two years of formal education, Benjamin Franklin was a brilliant polymath and inventor.

6

Benjamin Franklin Statue

📍H6 🏠Pennsylvania Ave & 10th St, NW Ⓜ Federal Triangle

Standing in front of the Old Post Office, this statue was unveiled by Franklin's great-granddaughter in 1889. The words "Printer, Philosopher, Patriot, Philanthropist" are inscribed on the four sides of the statue's pedestal. Postmaster General, writer, and scientist, Franklin was also a member of the committee that drafted the 1776 Declaration of Independence. As a diplomat to the court of Louis XVI of France, he went to Versailles in 1777 to gain support for the American cause of independence from Britain. Franklin returned to France in 1783 to negotiate the Treaty of Paris that ended the Revolutionary War.

7 🍴 🍽️

Willard Hotel

📍G6 🏠1401 Pennsylvania Ave, NW Ⓜ Metro Center 🌐washington. intercontinental.com

There has been a hotel on this site since 1816. Originally called Tennison's, the hotel occupied six adjacent two-story buildings. Refurbished in 1847, it was managed by Henry Willard, who gave his name to the hotel in 1850. Many famous people stayed here during the Civil War (1861–65), including Julia Ward Howe, who wrote the Civil War standard "The Battle Hymn of the Republic," and the writer Nathaniel Hawthorne. The word "lobbyist" is sometimes claimed to have been coined because it was known by those seeking favors that President Ulysses S. Grant went to the hotel's lobby to smoke his after-dinner cigar.

The present 330-room building was completed in 1904. It was the most popular place to stay in the city until the end of World War II, when the neighborhood fell into decline. For 20 years it was boarded up and faced demolition. A coalition worked to restore the Beaux Arts building, and it finally reopened in renewed splendor in 1986.

8 ♺ Ⓜ 💻 🛍️

National Museum of Women in the Arts

📍 H5 🏛️ 1250 New York Ave, NW Ⓜ Metro Center 🔒 For renovation until late 2023 🌐 nmwa.org

This museum of women's art houses works from the Renaissance to the present day. The superb collection was started in the 1960s by Wilhelmina Holladay and her husband, who picked up paintings, sculpture, and photography from all over the world. The museum operated out of their private residence for several years, until it acquired a more permanent home in this Renaissance Revival landmark building, formerly a Masonic Temple.

The collection's highlights include masterpieces by female American artists. Among the outstanding 19th-century works are *The Bath* (1891) by Mary Cassatt and *The Cage* (1885) by French artist Berthe Morisot. Among the works by 20th-century artists are Elizabeth Catlett's *Singing their Songs* (1992) and *Self-Portrait Between the Curtains, Dedication to Trotsky* (1937) by Mexican artist Frida Kahlo.

9

Pershing Park and National World War I Memorial

📍 GG 🏛️ Pennsylvania Ave & 15th St, NW Ⓜ Metro Center 🕐 24 hrs daily 🌐 nps.gov

Designed by renowned architect M. Paul Friedberg, Pershing Park opened in 1981 to commemorate World

←

Interior of Ford's Theatre, with the Presidential Box on the left

↓ *Les Trois Grâces* by Niki de Saint Phalle, National Museum of Women in the Arts

War I Commander of the American Expeditionary Forces John J. Pershing. After a number of years of falling into neglect, the park was converted into a National World War I Memorial in 2021. The statue of Pershing still stands within the park's American Expeditionary Forces Memorial. The main World War I memorial, with its massive bronze sculptural centerpiece *A Soldier's Journey* by New York sculptor Sabin Howard, is due to be completed in 2024.

10

National Theatre

📍 G6 🏛️ 1321 Pennsylvania Ave, NW Ⓜ Metro Center, Federal Triangle 🌐 thenationaldc.org

The National Theatre is the sixth theater to occupy this site and the oldest cultural institution in the city. The current building dates from 1922 and hosts Broadway-bound productions and touring groups. Known as an "actor's theater" because of its fine acoustics, the National is said to be haunted by the ghost of 19th-century actor John McCullough, killed by a fellow actor and buried under the stage.

EAT

Hill Country Barbecue Market
Authentic Texas BBQ joint known for its beef brisket, Hill Country jalapeño cheddar sausage, pulled pork, and ribs.

📍 J6 🏛️ 410 7th St, NW 🌐 hillcountry.com

💲💲💲

Oyamel Cocina Mexicana
Trendy, upscale restaurant serving creative Mexican small plates from chef José Andrés, with an extensive drinks menu.

📍 J6 🏛️ 401 7th St, NW 🌐 oyamel.com

💲💲💲

Zaytinya
Stylish restaurant with innovative Turkish, Greek, and Lebanese mezze dishes, and an immense wine list.

📍 H6 🏛️ 701 9th St, NW 🌐 zaytinya.com

💲💲💲

Daikaya Ramen
Busy little shop known for its authentic Japanese ramen noodles.

📍 J6 🏛️ 705 6th St, NW 🌐 daikaya.com

💲💲💲

Central Michel Richard
Modern American and French bistro with delightful entrees plus extensive drink menu.

📍 H6 🏛️ 1001 Pennsylvania Ave, NW 🌐 centralmichel richard.com

💲💲💲

11 Planet Word

📍H5 🏛925 13th St, NW
Ⓜ Metro Center 🕐10am-5pm Thu-Sun 🚫Jan 1, Thanksgiving, Dec 25
🌐planetwordmuseum.org

Opened in 2020 inside the impressive 1869 Franklin School, this museum celebrates language, with voice-activated exhibits and interactive galleries bringing words to life. The lobby is dominated by the *Speaking Willow* tree sculpture by contemporary artist Rafael Lozano-Hemmer, where recordings of hundreds of languages can be heard on loop. Other entertaining interactive displays explore the origins of words and the diversity of languages. Visitors can deliver famous speeches, paint a virtual wall with words, solve word puzzles, and even sing karaoke here.

STAY

W Washington DC

This elegant, upscale boutique hotel is set near the White House. Great views from the rooftop lounge.

📍G6 🏛515 15th St, NW
🌐marriott.com

$$$

Motto DC City Center

Small rooms, good beds, and essential amenities keep rates affordable. There's a diner, rooftop lounge, and free access to nearby fitness and shared workspaces.

📍J5 🏛627 H St, NW 🌐hilton.com

$$$

12 National Building Museum

📍J6 🏛401 F St at 4th St, NW Ⓜ Judiciary Square, Gallery Place-Chinatown 🕐10am-5pm Mon-Sat, 11am-5pm Sun 🚫Jan 1, Thanksgiving, Dec 25
🌐nbm.org

It is fitting that the National Building Museum, dedicated to the building trade, should be housed in the architecturally audacious former Pension Bureau building. It is based on Michelangelo's Palazzo Farnese, but is twice as big and in red brick as opposed to the stone masonry of the Rome original.

Completed in 1887, the vast concourse, measuring 316 ft by 116 ft (96 m by 35 m), is lined with balconies and has huge columns of plastered brick, faux-painted to give the appearance of marble. The Great Hall has been the venue for many presidential balls.

The building fell on hard times in the 1920s but was eventually restored, reopening in 1985 in renewed splendor as the National Building Museum. The museum features temporary exhibits on buildings and architecture, and a permanent exhibition on the architectural history of Washington, DC. For children under six, the "Building Zone" offers some hands-on fun, including giant LEGO blocks, bulldozers, and a playhouse.

13 Capital One Arena

📍J6 🏛601 F St, NW
Ⓜ Gallery Place-Chinatown 🕐10am-5:30pm daily, later on event days (team store)
🌐capitalonearena.com

Opened in 1997, the Capital One Arena is a sports and entertainment complex that houses many shops and restaurants. Its 20,000-seat stadium is the home of the city's basketball teams, the Wizards (men's team), the Mystics (women's), and the Georgetown Hoyas, as well as the ice hockey team, the Capitals. The presence of the complex has revived the surrounding area beyond recognition. It also hosts rock concerts as well as sports events and exhibitions.

14 Chinatown and H Street Corridor

📍J5 🏛Between 5th to 8th Sts & H to I St, NW Ⓜ Gallery Place-Chinatown

The small area in Washington, DC known as Chinatown covers just six square blocks. Formed around 1930, it has never been very large and today houses

→

A colorful dragon parade in Washington's Chinatown district

←

The huge columns of the National Building Museum concourse

about 500 Chinese residents. The area was reinvigorated with the arrival of the adjacent Capital One Arena in 1997.

The Friendship Archway, a dramatic gateway that spans H Street at the junction with 7th Street, marks the center of Chinatown. Built in 1986 as a gift from Beijing, it is the largest single-span Chinese arch in the world. During the Chinese New Year celebrations, the area comes alive with a colorful parade, dragon dances, and live musical performances (p42).

Chinatown is at the western end of a 1.5-mile (2.5-km) stretch of H Street that has undergone a remarkable revitalization. Multicultural neighborhoods have become incubators of a vibrant arts, music, and culinary scene, and the street is alive with shops, galleries, and restaurants. The anchor for this neighborhood is the historic Atlas Performing Arts Center, which stages award-winning shows.

DR. MARTIN LUTHER KING, JR.

A charismatic speaker, advocate of Gandhi's theories of nonviolence, and Nobel Peace Prize winner, Dr. King (1929–68) was a Black Baptist minister and civil rights leader. At the March on Washington in 1963, 200,000 people gathered at the Lincoln Memorial to hear King's "I Have a Dream" speech. Congress passed significant civil rights legislation the next year.

15

Martin Luther King Memorial Library

🗺 H6 🏠 901 G St at 9th St, NW Ⓜ Gallery Place-Chinatown, Metro Center 🕐 10am–6pm Mon–Wed, Fri & Sat, noon–8pm Thu, 1–5pm Sun 🌐 dclibrary.org/mlk

The Martin Luther King Memorial Library is the city's only example of the Modernist architecture of Ludwig Mies van der Rohe. A key figure in 20th-century design, van der Rohe finalized the library plans shortly before his death in 1969. It was named in honor of Dr. King when it opened in 1972, replacing the Carnegie Library as the city's central public library. Architecturally, the building is an austere, simple box with a recessed entrance lobby. Inside, there is a mural by artist Don Miller depicting Dr. King's life. The library sponsors numerous concerts and readings, as well as children's events.

A SHORT WALK
PENN QUARTER

Distance 1.2 miles (2 km) **Nearest Metro** Federal Triangle
Time 25 minutes

The main route for presidential inaugural parades, Pennsylvania Avenue is a grand boulevard worthy of L'Enfant's original vision. This spacious thoroughfare links the White House to the US Capitol and is home to some of the city's main sights. The Mellon Fountain is at the intersection with 6th Street, NW.

Opposite the US Navy Memorial is the US National Archives, housing original copies of the Constitution and the Declaration of Independence. Benjamin Franklin's statue stands in front of the Old Post Office, and the National Museum of Women in the Arts is on the corner of 12th Street, NW.

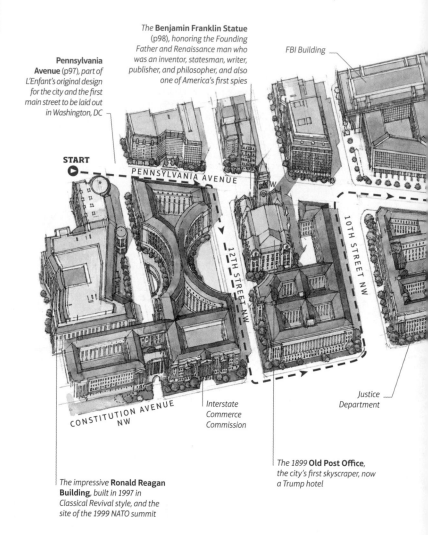

Pennsylvania **Avenue** (p97), *part of L'Enfant's original design for the city and the first main street to be laid out in Washington, DC*

The **Benjamin Franklin Statue** *(p98), honoring the Founding Father and Renaissance man who was an inventor, statesman, writer, publisher, and philosopher, and also one of America's first spies*

FBI Building

START

PENNSYLVANIA AVENUE

12TH STREET NW

10TH STREET NW

Justice Department

CONSTITUTION AVENUE NW

Interstate Commerce Commission

The 1899 **Old Post Office**, *the city's first skyscraper, now a Trump hotel*

The impressive **Ronald Reagan Building**, *built in 1997 in Classical Revival style, and the site of the 1999 NATO summit*

↑ The imposing United States Capitol seen from Pennsylvania Avenue

PENN QUARTER

Locator Map

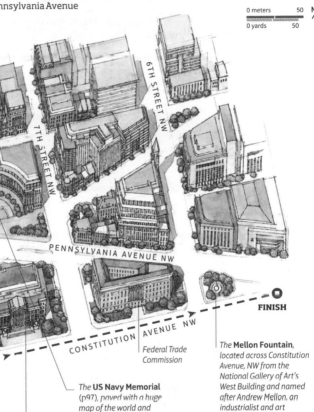

0 meters 50 N
0 yards 50 ↑

6TH STREET NW

7TH STREET NW

9TH STREET NW

PENNSYLVANIA AVENUE NW

CONSTITUTION AVENUE NW

FINISH

Federal Trade Commission

The **Mellon Fountain**, *located across Constitution Avenue, NW from the National Gallery of Art's West Building and named after Andrew Mellon, an industrialist and art collector who founded the gallery in the 1930s*

The **US Navy Memorial** *(p97), paved with a huge map of the world and surrounded by low granite walls, statuary, and fountains*

The **National Archives** *(p96), home to the nation's most precious documents, known as the Charters of Freedom*

→ The Neo-Classical building of the National Archives, designed by John Russell Pope in the early 1930s

The iconic south facade of the White House

WHITE HOUSE AND FOGGY BOTTOM

In 1800 the American government moved from Philadelphia to Washington, DC. At the time the city only had a scattering of simple buildings and mud streets. Nonetheless, John Adams and his wife Abigail took up residence in the new President's House, designed by James Hoban. Although burned down by the British during the War of 1812, most of today's building remains as it was planned and is still the heart of the area. West of the White House is the Foggy Bottom area. Built on swampland near the confluence of the Potomac and Rock Creek, it is said to have gained its name from the industries of the 19th century and an atmospheric quirk that funneled fog in. The area became home to George Washington University in the early 20th century, and also boasts the cutting-edge Kennedy Center, with its year-round calendar of celebrated performances.

WHITE HOUSE AND FOGGY BOTTOM

Must See

1 White House

Experience More

2 Lafayette Square
3 Treasury Building
4 Hay-Adams Hotel
5 St. John's Church
6 Renwick Gallery
7 Octagon House Museum
8 Textile Museum and GWU Museum
9 George Washington University
10 Organization of American States
11 National Geographic Museum
12 Watergate Complex
13 The Kennedy Center

Eat

① El Chalan
② GCDC Grilled Cheese Bar
③ CIRCA

Stay

④ Hotel Hive
⑤ Mayflower Hotel

① ⊗ ☐

WHITE HOUSE

📍 G6 🏠 White House: 1600 Pennsylvania Ave, NW; visitor center: 1450 Pennsylvania Ave, NW Ⓜ Federal Triangle 🕐 White House: Fri & Sat; visitor center: 7:30am–4pm daily ❌ White House: Federal holidays, official functions; visitor center: Jan 1, Thanksgiving, Dec 25 🌐 nps.gov/whho

With every US president except George Washington having called the White House home, this Neo-Classical mansion has been the seat of executive power for over 200 years.

One of the most famous residential landmarks in the world, the White House was built to reflect the power of the presidency. Although George Washington commissioned the mansion, President John Adams was its first occupant, in 1800. In 1902, President Theodore Roosevelt ordered the West Wing to be built, and in 1942 the East Wing was added by President Franklin D. Roosevelt, completing the building as it is today.

TOP 5 DECORATIVE FEATURES

China Room Collection
A collection of family and state china from nearly every president.

Monroe Plateau
A 14.5-ft- (4.5-m-) long French gilt table service.

Grand Staircase
Used for ceremonial entrances and presidential portraits.

North Entrance Carvings
Finely made door surround carved with flowing garlands of roses and acorns.

Vermeil Room
A display of "vermeil," gilded objects by 19th-century silversmiths, and several portraits of First Ladies.

→

The White House facade, and the Diplomatic Reception room *(inset)*, with its famous Zuber "Views of North America" block printed wallpaper

Timeline

1792

△ George Washington approves the design of the mansion. Completed in 1800, it is burned down in 1814 by the British during the War of 1812.

1901

△ The structure is renamed the White House by Theodore Roosevelt; his successor, William Taft *(above)*, creates the first Oval Office in 1909.

1948

△ Harry Truman begins a major reconstruction of the building in which absolutely everything except the outer walls is dismantled.

2013

△ Barack Obama installs solar panels on the roof, the first time solar power is used for a president's living quarters.

Did You Know?

570 gallons (2,100 liters) of paint are needed to cover the exterior of the White House.

Exploring the White House

The 132 rooms in the White House, decorated in period styles and filled with antique furniture, china, and silverware, preserve the cultural and political touchstones of America's past and present. Hanging on their walls are some of America's most treasured paintings, including portraits of past presidents and First Ladies. To tour the White House, you must start the process well before your visit. US citizens must request tickets from their Member of Congress. The request can be made up to three months in advance, but tickets must be requested at least 21 days in advance. Foreign citizens must make a request for tickets at their embassy in DC (tickets for non-US citizens are difficult to come by). Those without tour tickets can experience a virtual tour at the White House Visitor Center.

The West Terrace, leading to the West Wing and the Oval Office, the president's official office

→

The White House, both a presidential residence and a working office building

The State Dining Room, enlarged in 1902 and able to seat as many as 140 people

The Red Room, one of three reception rooms on the State Floor, furnished in the Empire Style (1810–30)

FLIPPING THE WHITE HOUSE

On Inauguration Day, the White House must be changed over for the incoming president in just five hours. At 10:30am the outgoing family leaves for the inauguration, and the carefully choreographed chaos begins. The outgoing family's moving trucks park on the South Portico's west side, and the incoming family's on the east. The rooms are scrubbed, rugs and curtains cleaned, repairs made, all personal belongings placed, and the Oval Office painted. At 3:30pm the new First Family arrives, and the Chief Usher says, "Welcome to your new home, Mr. President."

The Lincoln Bedroom, used by President Lincoln as his Cabinet Room

The East Terrace, leading to the East Wing, which houses offices rather than ceremonial rooms

The Treaty Room, which served as the Cabinet Room for ten presidents starting with Andrew Johnson in 1865

The East Room, used for large gatherings such as concerts and press conferences

The Vermeil Room, housing six paintings of First Ladies

The Green Room, first used by Thomas Jefferson as a dining room

The Blue Room, the most elegant of the reception rooms

The Diplomatic Reception room, furnished in Federal style (1790–1820)

Did You Know?

The White House has 412 doors, 147 windows, 132 rooms, 35 bathrooms, 28 fireplaces, and 8 staircases.

1 Every president personalizes the Oval Office - Obama added a bust of Martin Luther King, Jr., while Biden added a bust of labor organizer and civil rights leader César Chávez.

2 The State Dining Room mantel has a portrait of President Lincoln.

3 The Red Room, decorated by Jacqueline Kennedy, is used as a sitting room and for small parties.

EXPERIENCE MORE

② Lafayette Square

📍G6 🅼Farragut West,
McPherson Sq 🌐nps.gov

Behind the White House is
Lafayette Square, named
for the Marquis de Lafayette
(1757–1834), who fought in the
Revolutionary War. This park
is home to 19th-century mansions and the historic St. John's,
"Church of the Presidents."
In the center is a huge statue
of President Andrew Jackson
(1767–1845), and at its four
corners stand statues of men
who took part in America's
struggle for liberty. The southeast corner honors Lafayette.
In the southwest is Jean-
Baptiste Donatien de Vimeur,
Comte de Rochambeau (1725–
1807). Baron von Steuben
(1730–94), Washington's aide
at Valley Forge, is honored in
the northwest end. Polish
general Tadeusz Kościuszko
(1746–1817), who fought in the
Revolutionary War, stands
in the northeast.

↑ A bronze seal from 1789
on display at the
Treasury Building

③ Treasury Building

📍G6 🏛Pennsylvania Ave
& 15th St, NW 🅼McPherson
Square 🕐Sat for guided
tours only for citizens and
legal residents of the US
(register in advance with
your Congressional Office)
🌐treasury.gov

This grand four-story Greek
Revival edifice was designed
by architect Robert Mills, who
also designed the Washington

Monument (p83). The official
guided tour takes in the
restored historic rooms, including the 1864 burglar-proof
vault and the marble Cash
Room. Between 1863 and 1880,
US currency was printed in the
basement. Today, the building
is home to the Department of
the Treasury, which manages
the government's finances and
protects US financial systems.

④ 🍴 🍷 Hay-Adams Hotel

📍F5 🏛1 Lafayette Sq, NW
🅼Farragut North, Farragut
West 🌐hayadams.com

Situated close to the
White House, this historic
hotel is a city landmark built
in Italian Renaissance style
and with an interior adorned
with beautiful European
antiques. It has been a
popular hotel since its
1927 conversion and remains
one of Washington's top
establishments, well sited

BLACK LIVES MATTER PLAZA

Following the murder of a Black American
named George Floyd by a white police
officer in Minneapolis on May 5, 2020,
peaceful Black Lives Matter (BLM) protests
took place in DC and all around the world.
On June 1, federal officers broke up a BLM
protest in DC, just north of the White
House, with violence and tear gas. In the
aftermath, on June 5, a section of 16th

Street, between H Street at Lafayette Park
and K Street, was officially renamed Black
Lives Matter Plaza by DC Mayor Muriel
Bowser. This two-block pedestrianized
zone between Hay-Adams Hotel and
St. John's Church is now a public gathering
place, with the words "Black Lives Matter"
painted on the street in 35-ft- (11-m-) tall
yellow capital letters as a permanent mural.

↑ An elegant interior in the Octagon House Museum, restored to its 1815 appearance

EAT

El Chalan

Authentic Peruvian cuisine served in a cozy dining room.

📍E5 🏠1924 I St, NW
🕐Sun & L Sat
🌐elchalandc.com

$$$

GCDC Grilled Cheese Bar

Near the White House, this restaurant serves grilled cheese sand wiches, including the French onion and buffalo blue.

📍F6 🏠1730 Pennsylvania Ave, NW
🕐Sun & from 6pm Sat
🌐grilledcheesedc.com

$$⑤

CIRCA

Trendy bistro with creative New American fare and drinks.

📍E5 🏠2221 I St, NW
🌐circabistros.com

$$$

---

for all the major sights. Drop in for afternoon tea at the Lafayette Restaurant.

5

St. John's Church

📍G5 🏠16th & H Sts, NW at Lafayette Sq Ⓜ McPherson Square 🕐1–3pm daily
🌐stjohns-dc.org

This graceful, historic church has hosted every sitting

←
The iconic Black Lives Matter Plaza, Downtown DC

US president since James Madison. Built in 1816, it has a simple yet elegant interior with 22 beautiful stained-glass memorial windows. A guided tour is offered after the 11am service on Sunday.

6

Renwick Gallery

📍F6 🏠Pennsylvania Ave at 17th St, NW
Ⓜ Farragut West
🕐10am–5:30pm daily
🕐Labor Day & Dec 25
🌐americanart.si.edu

Part of the Smithsonian American Art Museum (p92), this elegant redbrick building was designed and constructed by James Renwick Jr. in 1858.

The gallery's mission is to conserve and display the Smithsonian's collection of 20th-century and contemporary American arts, crafts, and design. Highlights of the collection include superb examples of American craftsmanship, such as master woodworker Wendell Castle's *Ghost Clock*, a wooden piece that looks like a grandfather clock draped in delicate linen, and Larry Fuente's *Game Fish*, a large sculptural sailfish that is encrusted with toy and game pieces such as dice and ping-pong balls.

7

Octagon House Museum

📍F6 🏠1799 New York Ave, NW Ⓜ Farragut West, Farragut North 🕐1–4pm Thu–Sat 🕐Jan 1, Thanksgiving, Dec 25
🌐architectsfoundation. org/octagon-museum

Actually hexagonal in shape, the Octagon is a three-story redbrick building designed in the late-Federal style by Dr. William Thornton (1759–1828), first architect of the US Capitol. It was completed in 1801 for Colonel John Tayloe III, a plantation owner and a friend of George Washington. After the White House was burned down in the War of 1812 against Britain, President James Madison and his wife Dolley lived here from 1814 to 1815.

Octagon House has been fully restored to its historically accurate 1815 appearance and now houses an architectural museum run by the American Institute of Architects. Visitors can take self-guided tours, and unlike most other fine home museums, here they are encouraged to touch and use furnishings, lie on the rope bed, or play a game of whist in the drawing room. The house is full of architectural features, including an impressive circular entrance hall. Admission is free but there is a suggested donation of $10.

Artifacts on display at the Textile Museum, including shoes *(inset)*, garments, and fabric ↑

8

Textile Museum and GWU Museum

QE6 **⌂**701 21st St, NW **M**Foggy Bottom-GWU, Farragut North **⊙**10am-5pm Wed-Fri **⊗**University hols **W**museum.gwu.edu

This unusual museum has one of the world's finest collections of rugs, tapestries, and textiles spanning over 5,000 years. Created in 1929 by George Hewitt Myers, the collection has over 21,000 items, including 15th-century Mamluk carpets from Egypt and Native American weavings dating back to 900 BC. There is also a library featuring 20,000 publications on textiles.

The George Washington University Museum (part of the same complex) has the Albert H. Small Washingtoniana collection of artworks, publications, and artifacts that relate the city's history from pre-Revolutionary times to the present.

9

George Washington University

QE5 **⌂**2121 I (Eye) St, NW **M**Foggy Bottom-GWU **W**gwu.edu

Founded in 1821, George Washington university, known as "GW," is named after the first US president. The largest university in DC, it has nine schools offering both undergraduate and graduate studies.

As a result of its location, GW has many famous alumni, including General Colin Powell (Secretary of State in George W. Bush's administration) and Jacqueline Bouvier (who married John Kennedy) as well as many children of past presidents. On-campus auditoriums host plays, dances, lectures, and concerts.

10

Organization of American States

QF7 **⌂**Corner of 17th St & Constitution Ave **M**Farragut West **⊗**Federal hols

Dating back to the First International Conference of the American States, held from October 1889 to April 1890 in Washington, DC, the Organization of American States (OAS) is the oldest alliance of nations devoted to reinforcing the continent's peace and security and maintaining democracy. The Charter of the OAS was signed in 1948 in Bogotá, Colombia, by the US and 20 Latin American republics. Today there are 35 members. The grounds contain the **Art Museum of the Americas** and the **Columbus Memorial Library**, which exhibits 20th-century Latin American and Caribbean art.

Art Museum of the Americas

⌂201 18th St, NW **⊙**10am-5pm Tue-Sun **⊗**Good Friday, Federal hols **W**museum.oas.org

Columbus Memorial Library

⌂19th St & Constitution Ave **⊙**Times vary, check website **W**oas.org

11

National Geographic Museum

QF4 **⌂**1145 17th St, NW **M**Farragut North, Farragut West **⊙**10am-6pm daily **⊗**Thanksgiving, Dec 25 **W**nationalgeographic.org

This small museum is located in the National Geographic Society's headquarters, designed by Edward Durrell Stone, the architect behind the Kennedy Center.

Exhibitions here document the richness of nature and the diversity of human culture all over the world.

12

Watergate Complex

D6 **Virginia Ave between Rock Creek Pkwy & New Hampshire Ave, NW** **Foggy Bottom-GWU** **thewatergatehotel.com**

Next to the Kennedy Center, the impressive Watergate Complex was completed in 1971. Its four rounded buildings contain offices, apartments, hotels, shops, and diplomatic missions.

In 1972 the complex was at the center of international news when burglars, linked to President Nixon, broke into the Democratic National Committee offices, sparking the Watergate scandal that led to the president's resignation.

The stunning Watergate Hotel has turned the infamous room 214 into a luxury room, aka Scandal Room, and a museum. For a price varying between $1,000 and $2,500

a night, guests can sleep in the actual room from which the 1972 break-in was supervised.

13

The Kennedy Center

D6 **New Hampshire Ave & Rock Creek Pkwy, NW** **Foggy Bottom-GWU** **10am–6pm Mon–Wed (to 9pm Thu & Fri), noon–9pm Sat & Sun** **kennedy-center.org**

In 1958, President Dwight D. Eisenhower signed an act to begin fundraising for a national cultural center that would attract the world's best orchestras, opera, and dance companies to the US capital. President John F. Kennedy was an ardent supporter of the arts, taking the lead in fundraising for it. He never saw the completion of the center, which was named in his honor.

Designed by Edward Durrell Stone, the center houses several theaters: the Opera House, the Concert Hall, the Eisenhower Theater, and the Family Theater. On the roof

are the Terrace Theater and the Theater Lab. In 2018, the center added The Reach to its riverfront area. This complex hosts the Millennium Stage, which presents free, family-friendly performances over the summer, as well as a jazz venue, The Club at Studio K.

The Opera House seats over 2,300 people. The vast chandelier is made of Lobmeyr crystal and was a gift from Austria.

Flags of the 50 US states, five territories, and the District of Columbia hang in the Hall of States.

The Hall of Nations houses the flag of every country with which the US has diplomatic relations.

The Concert Hall is the largest auditorium, with more than 2,400 seats. It is home to the National Symphony Orchestra.

A bust of President Eisenhower by Felix de Weldon hangs in Eisenhower Theater's lobby.

The JFK Terrace stretches the length of the center and has glorious river views. Quotes by John F. Kennedy are engraved into the walls.

The bust of JFK in the Grand Foyer was created by sculptor Robert Berks.

The grand John F. Kennedy Center for the Performing Arts

The Reach

The Grand Foyer stretches 630 ft (192 m) and is an impressive entrance into the Opera House, the Concert Hall, and the Eisenhower Theater.

A SHORT WALK

AROUND THE
WHITE HOUSE

Distance 2 miles (3 km) **Nearest Metro** McPherson Square **Time** 35 minutes

The area surrounding the White House is filled with grand architecture and political history, and the vistas from the Ellipse lawn are breathtaking. The nearby Octagon House was built in 1801 for Colonel John Tayloe, and St. John's Church opened in 1816 when James Madison was president. The Renwick Gallery now occupies the first building in the nation that was built to be a museum, but before it was completed it was used by the Union Army during the Civil War. The building opened as the Corcoran School of the Arts & Design in 1874. Nearby is the Eisenhower Executive Office Building, which was the world's largest office building when it opened in 1888.

The **Renwick Gallery** (p113), with an inscription above the entrance reading "Dedicated to Art"

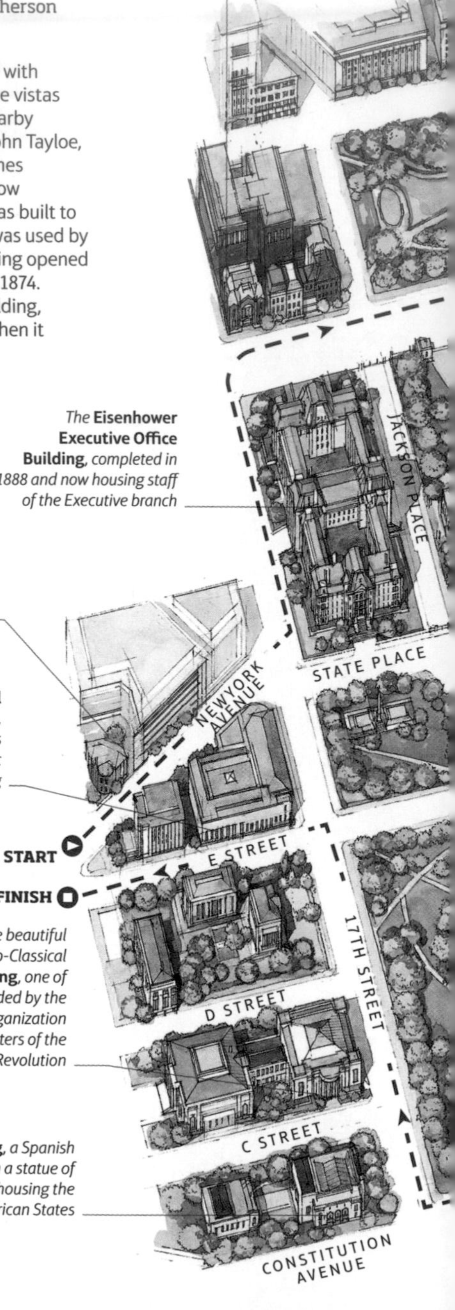

The **Eisenhower Executive Office Building**, completed in 1888 and now housing staff of the Executive branch

The **Octagon Museum** (p113), at various times the home of fourth US president James Madison, a hospital, and a school

The **Corcoran School of the Arts & Design**, which hosts exhibitions and events in its historic Flagg Building

START

FINISH

Did You Know?

The Ellipse was used for baseball games from the 1860s onward and is still used for amateur sports.

The beautiful Neo-Classical **DAR Building**, one of three founded by the historical organization the Daughters of the American Revolution

The 1910 **OAS Building**, a Spanish Colonial-style mansion, with a statue of Isabella of Spain outside, housing the Organization of American States

JACKSON PLACE · STATE PLACE · NEW YORK AVENUE · E STREET · 17TH STREET · D STREET · C STREET · CONSTITUTION AVENUE

The luxurious **Hay-Adams Hotel** (p112), the scene of political activity since it opened in the 1920s

St. John's Church (p123), known as the "Church of Presidents" as every president since James Madison has attended services here

Locator Map
For more detail see p108

Leafy **Lafayette Square** (p112), named after the Revolutionary War officer the Marquis de Lafayette

The **White House** (p108), one of the most famous sights in Washington, DC and the US president's official residence since the 1800s

Treasury Building

↑ The Treasury Building, built over 33 years and widely regarded as one of the most impressive Neo-Classical structures in the city

The **Ellipse**, site of the annual National Christmas Tree (p43) and the Zero Milestone from which all DC distances are measured

THE ELLIPSE

0 meters   100
0 yards   100

N ↑

Vine-covered walls of the Orangery at Dumbarton Oaks

GEORGETOWN

The Indigenous, Algonquian-speaking Nacotchtank peoples
who lived along the southeast side of the Anacostia River
founded a major trading village on this site in the 17th
century. The arrival of Europeans soon after was deadly
for the Indigenous population: by 1700, all had perished
from European diseases or been driven out by colonists.
In 1703 a land grant was given to Ninian Beall, who named
the area the Rock of Dumbarton. By the mid-18th century
immigrants from Scotland had swelled the population, and in
1751 the town was renamed George Town. It grew rapidly into
a wealthy tobacco and flour port and finally, in 1789, the city
of Georgetown was formed. The harbor and the Chesapeake
and Ohio Canal were built in 1828, and the streets were
lined with townhouses. The birth of the railroad undercut
Georgetown's economy, which by the mid-1800s was in
decline. But by the 1950s the cobblestoned streets and
charming houses were attracting wealthy young couples,
and restaurants and shops sprang up on Wisconsin Avenue
and M Street. Today Georgetown retains its sophisticated
distinction from the rest of the city, and is a pleasant area
in which to stroll for a few hours.

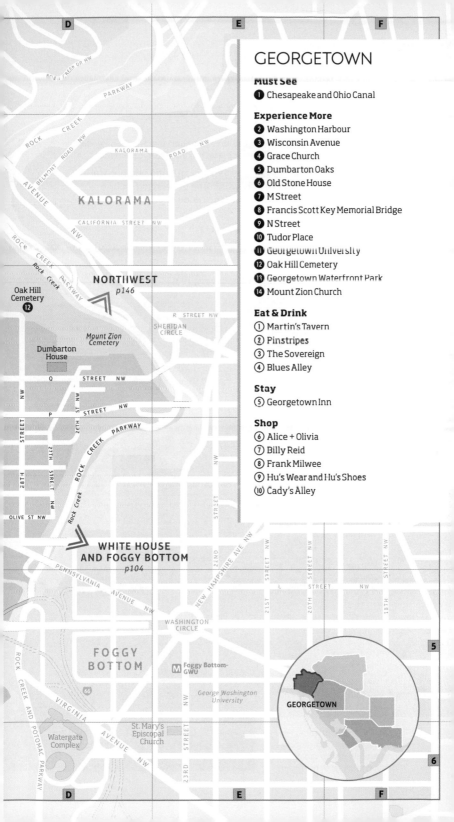

GEORGETOWN

Must See
❶ Chesapeake and Ohio Canal

Experience More
❷ Washington Harbour
❸ Wisconsin Avenue
❹ Grace Church
❺ Dumbarton Oaks
❻ Old Stone House
❼ M Street
❽ Francis Scott Key Memorial Bridge
❾ N Street
❿ Tudor Place
⓫ Georgetown University
⓬ Oak Hill Cemetery
⓭ Georgetown Waterfront Park
⓮ Mount Zion Church

Eat & Drink
① Martin's Tavern
② Pinstripes
③ The Sovereign
④ Blues Alley

Stay
⑤ Georgetown Inn

Shop
⑥ Alice + Olivia
⑦ Billy Reid
⑧ Frank Milwee
⑨ Hu's Wear and Hu's Shoes
⑩ Cady's Alley

CHESAPEAKE AND OHIO CANAL

📍C5 🚪From 29th & M Sts, NW in Georgetown to Cumberland, MD Ⓜ Foggy Bottom-GWU, then 15-min walk 🚌31, 33 🕐Sunrise-sunset daily 🌐nps.gov/choh

The 184-mile (296-km) Chesapeake and Ohio Canal National Historical Park attracts over five million visitors who come to walk, jog, or bike along the towpath, canoe or kayak along the canal, or just enjoy the park's natural beauty.

Constructed between 1828 and 1850, the Chesapeake and Ohio Canal (C&O Canal) connected Georgetown to the rich farmlands of Cumberland, Maryland, and incorporated a revolutionary system of locks, aqueducts, and tunnels that allowed inland farmers to ship their produce quickly to eastern cities. With the arrival of the railroad in the late 19th century, the canal fell out of use, and became a national park in 1971. The most popular section is the 3-mile (5-km) stretch from M Street to Fletcher's Boathouse, with picnic areas, great fishing, and boat rentals, and historic Abner Cloud House just across the towpath. Great Falls is also popular, with hiking and canal boat rides.

Did You Know?

A gongoozler is someone who likes to sit and idly watch the activity on a canal.

The serene canal, with costumed guides offering 19th-century-style mule-drawn canal boat rides on some stretches *(inset)* ↑

[1] The easiest way to enjoy the park is to walk, jog, or cycle along the canal towpath through Georgetown and west to Fletcher's Boathouse.

[2] The Potomac creates a dramatic sight as it cascades through rocky Mather Gorge at Great Falls. Visitors come to hike the trails, take a canal boat ride, and learn about the history.

[3] Canoeing and kayaking are popular on the C&O and are best between Georgetown and Violette's Lock – the first 22 miles (35 km) of the canal.

GEORGE'S CANAL

George Washington was the first to see the potential of linking the Potomac and the Ohio River Valley to transport goods. After his presidency, he set up the Patowmack Company, which built skirting canals around Great Falls. The project was completed after his death, and was superseded 26 years later by the C&O Canal.

↑ Patowmack Canal cargo toll cards

EXPERIENCE MORE

② Washington Harbour

C5 🏠 3000-3020 K St, NW Ⓜ Foggy Bottom-GWU, then 15-min walk 🌐 the washingtonharbour.com

Washington Harbour architect Arthur Cotton Moore created an unusually audacious development on the Potomac in 1981, with five large residential and commercial buildings that tower above the waterfront and surround a large open plaza ringed with shops and restaurants. The plaza also features a huge fountain that becomes a popular ice-skating rink in winter.

This is a great place to walk along the pleasant waterfront boardwalk, to dine inside or outside overlooking the water, or just sit and watch boats of all types make their way along the Potomac. A walkway follows the river and leads to the adjacent Georgetown Waterfront Park. The area's popularity and success eventually set the stage for much larger developments like District Wharf (*p136*) and National Harbor (*p173*) that have lately revitalized the city's waterfront areas.

Did You Know?

Wisconsin Avenue follows an ancient Native American trail, and first appeared on a map in 1712.

③ Wisconsin Avenue

C4 🏠 Wisconsin Ave Ⓜ Foggy Bottom-GWU

Wisconsin Avenue is one of two main business streets in Georgetown and is home to a wide variety of trendsetting shops and restaurants. It is also one of the few streets in Washington, DC that predates L'Enfant's grid plan. It starts at the bank of the Potomac and runs north through Georgetown right to the city line, where it continues as Rockville Pike. On the junction of Wisconsin Avenue and M Street is the landmark gold dome of PNC Bank (formerly the Farmers and Mechanics National Bank). During the French and Indian Wars, George Washington marched his troops up the avenue on his way to Pittsburgh to engage the French forces.

④ Grace Church

C5 🏠 1041 Wisconsin Ave, NW Ⓜ Foggy Bottom-GWU, Rosslyn, then 20-min walk 🕙 10am–4pm Mon–Fri, 8am–noon & 5–6:30pm Sun 🌐 gracedc.org

Built in 1866, Grace Church was designed to serve the boatmen who worked on the Chesapeake and Ohio Canal (*p122*) and the sailors of the port of Georgetown. Set on a tree-filled plot south of the canal and M Street, the Gothic Revival church, with its quaint exterior, is an oasis of calm in Georgetown. As the building has undergone few alterations over the years, it has a certain timeless quality. The church's multiethnic congregation makes great efforts to reach out to the larger DC community and works with soup kitchens and shelters for the homeless. In addition, the church holds concerts on the lawn on Thursdays (5:30–7pm) in September and several times a year after

Washington Harbour ↓

↑ Lush fig plants among the abundant greenery in the Orangery at Dumbarton Oaks

the Sunday service. Classical concerts, including chamber pieces, organ, and piano works, are held regularly There is also a popular annual festival in July devoted to German composer J. S. Bach.

5 ⊘ Ⓜ 🖐

Dumbarton Oaks

🔲 C2 🏠 1703 32nd St, NW Ⓜ Foggy Bottom-GWU, Dupont Circle, then bus 🕐 House: 11:30am–5pm Tue–Sun; gardens: 3–6pm Tue–Sun (to 5pm Nov–Feb) 🔒 Federal hols 🔲 doaks.org

Originally built in 1801 by Senator William Dorsey of Maryland, this fine Federal-style home was overgrown and neglected when it was purchased by pharmaceutical heirs Robert and Mildred Woods Bliss in 1920. The Blisses lovingly restored and modernized the house to meet 20th-century family needs. They also wanted their home to be surrounded by superb gardens, so they engaged their friend, Beatrix Jones Farrand, one of the few female landscape architects at the time, to lay out the grounds. Farrand's design began with lush formal gardens close to the house,

and slowly became less structured farther away, eventually blending in with the surrounding woodlands.

The Blisses were also avid collectors of Byzantine art, and in 1940, when they moved to California, they donated their whole estate to Harvard University. It was then converted into a library, research institution, and museum, where many of the pieces on display are those collected by the Blisses. Greco-Roman coins, late Roman and early Byzantine bas-reliefs, Roman glass and bronzeware, and Egyptian fabrics are just a few of the highlights. In 1962 Robert Bliss donated his collection of pre-Columbian art, which required a specially designed wing to be added to the house. It includes masks and gold jewelry from Central America, and Aztec carvings.

Visitors to the gardens today can explore room after outdoor room of lovely land-scaped spaces and flower gardens. There is a stunning walled rose garden, a fountain terrace, a wonderfully romantic 1930s-style swimming pool, and a formal boxwood garden, among others. Winding paths lead from one secret nook to another, lending a sense of mystery and wonder to the exploration.

EAT & DRINK

Martin's Tavern
A celebrated restaurant where JFK proposed to his wife Jackie.

🔲 C4 🏠 1264 Wisconsin Ave, NW 🔲 martins tavern.com

($)($)($)

Pinstripes
Italian American bistro with ample room for bowling and bocce (a type of boules).

🔲 C4 🏠 1064 Wisconsin Ave, NW 🔲 pinstripes.com

($)($)($)

The Sovereign
Wonderful Belgian beers and food served in an attractive gastropub.

🔲 C4 🏠 1206 Wisconsin Ave, NW 🔲 the sovereignc.com

($)($)($)

Blues Alley
Intimate jazz club with live performances and potent drinks.

🔲 C4 🏠 1073 Wisconsin Ave, NW 🔲 bluesalley.com

($)($)($)

6

Old Stone House

📍 C4 🏠 3051 M St, NW
Ⓜ Foggy Bottom-GWU, then
15-min walk 🚌 30, 32, 34,
36, 38 🕙 11am–7pm daily
🌐 nps.gov/rocr

Possibly the only building in
Washington, DC that predates
the American Revolution, the
Old Stone House was built in
1765 by Christopher Layman,
and is now a welcome respite
from the busy M Street.

A legend that still persists
about the Old Stone House is
that it was the Suter's Tavern
where Washington and Pierre
L'Enfant made their plans for
the city. However, most his-
torians today believe that
they met in a tavern located
elsewhere in Georgetown.

Over the years, the building
has housed a series of
artisans, and in the 1950s it
served as offices for a used-
car dealership. In 1960 the
National Park Service restored
it to its pre-Revolutionary War
appearance. Today, the house
serves as a Rock Creek Park
(p171) visitor center and store,
and holds a small museum
that charts its long history.
The Old Stone House is tech-
nically the oldest house in DC,
although the Lindens, now in
Kalorama, was built in the mid-
1750s in Massachusetts and
later moved to Washington, DC.

7

M Street

📍 C4 🏠 M St, NW Ⓜ Foggy
Bottom-GWU, then 15-min
walk 🚌 30, 32, 34, 36, 38

One of Georgetown's two main
shopping streets, M Street is
also home to some of the

most historic spots in the city.
On the northeast corner of
30th and M streets, on the
current site of a bank, stood
Union Tavern. Built in 1796,
it played host to, among
others, presidents George
Washington and John Adams,
author Washington Irving, and
Francis Scott Key, composer of
"The Star-Spangled Banner."
During the Civil War, the inn
was turned into a temporary
hospital where Louisa May
Alcott, author of *Little Women*,
nursed wounded soldiers.

William Thornton, architect
of the US Capitol and Tudor
Place (p130), lived at 3219 M
Street. On the south side of
the street at number 3276 is
Market House, which has been
the location of Georgetown's
market since 1751. A wood
frame market house was built
in 1796 and replaced by the
current brick market in 1865.
In the 1930s the market
became an auto supply store.

Today M Street and the
adjacent blocks are home to
stores and restaurants. Line up
for sweet treats at Georgetown
Cupcake or bubble tea at
Gong Cha Georgetown, and
shop at places such as Urban
Outfitters, Anthropologie,
CB2 or Alice + Olivia. The
fashionable Cady's Alley,
at 3318 M Street, is a haven
of trendy boutiques and
high-end furnishing stores.
Clyde's restaurant at 3236
is a Georgetown institution,
famous for its happy hour;
Kafe Leopold on Cady's
Alley offers a shaded patio
where you can sit, sip coffee,

Interior *(inset)* and
exterior of the Old Stone
House, possibly DC's
oldest building

↑ Georgetown's popular M Street, with a variety of stores and restaurants

enjoy Austrian specialties, and watch the people of Georgetown go by.

---

⑧

Frances Scott Key Memorial Bridge

📍B5 🕐24 hours daily

Gorgeous and stately, the oldest surviving road bridge across the Potomac River is named after poet Frances Scott Key (1779-1843), who penned the US national anthem. At the time of its completion in 1923, he lived just a few blocks from its north abutment. The Francis Key Scott Memorial is a park and memorial located next to the bridge at 34th and M Street, with a bronze bust as well as exhibits explaining the poet's story.

The busy, eight-arch, six-lane, 1,791 ft (546 m) reinforced concrete bridge conveys traffic between Rosslyn in Arlington, Virginia, and Georgetown. With pedestrian and bike paths, it buzzes with locals as well as tourists enjoying the neighborhoods' upscale restaurants, bars, and shops. The **Key Bridge Boathouse** on the shore rents canoes, kayaks, and paddleboards by the hour.

Guided tours to the Lincoln Memorial take guests along the waterfront, past Theodore Roosevelt Island and provide a stunning view of the monuments while gliding on the calm river.

Key Bridge Boathouse

🚶 📍C4 🏠3500 Water St, NW Ⓜ Rosslyn, Foggy Bottom-GWU, then 25-min walk 🕐Apr-Nov: daily 🌐boating indc.com/boathouses/key-bridge-boathouse

---

⑨

N Street

📍C4 🏠N St, NW Ⓜ Foggy Bottom-GWU, then 15-min walk 🚌30, 32, 34, 36

N Street is lined with beautiful 18th century American Federal row houses. This style was favored by leaders of the new nation as being of a more refined design than the earlier Georgian architecture. At the corner of 30th and N streets at number 3014 is the Laird-Dunlop House. It was once the home of the former editor of the *Washington Post* Benjamin Bradlee and his wife Sally Quinn. An excellent example of a Federal house is the Riggs- Riley House at 3038 N Street, once owned by diplomats and socialites Averill and Pamela Harriman. At 3041–3045 is Wheatley Row, houses built above street level with large windows, offering maximum light but also maximum privacy. The house at 3307 is where the Kennedys lived before moving to the White House.

1770

The oldest surviving house on N Street, 3033, was built by mayor Thomas Beall.

SHOP

Alice + Olivia

Hip, upscale boutique with chic women's fashions and accessories for all occasions.

📍B4 🏠3303 M St, NW 🌐aliceandolivia.com

Billy Reid

Antiques-filled store showcasing the Alabama-based designer's vintage rock chic.

📍C4 🏠3211 M St, NW 🌐billyreid.com

Frank Milwee

Browse a quality selection of antiques, with silver, home decor, and unusual items at this M Street store. Don't miss the corkscrews.

📍C4 🏠2912 M St, NW ☎(202) 333-4811

Hu's Wear and Hu's Shoes

Local style guru Marlene Hu Aldaba curates her two shops with stylish and bold fashion pieces, plus an on-trend selection of handbags and accessories.

📍D4 🏠2906 M St, NW 🌐husonline.com

Cady's Alley

An irresistible cluster of high-end fashion, jewelry, design, and home furnishing shops located on the south side of M Street.

📍B4 🏠3314 M St, NW 🌐cadysalley.com

10
Tudor Place

📍 C3 🏛 1644 31st St, NW Ⓜ Dupont Circle, Foggy Bottom-GWU, then bus 🕐 10am–4pm Tue–Sat, noon–4pm Sun 🎫 Check website 🌐 tudorplace.org

The manor house and large gardens of this Georgetown estate, designed by British-American physician, inventor, painter, and architect William Thornton (1759–1828), who also designed the Capitol, offer a unique glimpse into a bygone era.

Martha Washington, the wife of George Washington and America's first First Lady, gave $8,000 to her granddaughter, Martha Custis Peter, and her granddaughter's husband, Thomas Peter. With the money, they purchased 8 acres (3.2 ha) and commissioned Thornton to design a grand house. Six generations of the Peters family lived here from 1805 to 1984. It is something of a mystery as to why this stuccoed, two-story Georgian structure with a "temple" porch is called Tudor Place, but it was perhaps illustrative of the English sympathies held by the family at that time. The furniture,

silver, china, and portraits in Tudor Place provide a glimpse into American social and cultural history; some of the pieces on display come from Mount Vernon (*p162*).

Outside, 5.5 acres (2.2 ha) of formal gardens and picturesque woodland spaces can be explored along pretty stone paths.

11
Georgetown University

📍 B4 🏛 37th & O Sts, NW Ⓜ Rosslyn, then bus 🌐 georgetown.edu

Georgetown University was the first Catholic college to be established in America. Founded in 1789 by John Carroll, and affiliated with the Jesuit Order, the university now attracts students of all faiths from more than 100 countries around the world.

The oldest building on the campus is the Old North Building, completed in 1872. However, the most recognizable structure is the Healy Building, a Germanic design topped by a fanciful spiral. The university's most famous graduate is former US president Bill Clinton.

INSIDER TIP
Kayak the Potomac

Rent kayaks, canoes, or sculls at the Thompson Boat Center at 2900 Virginia Avenue, NW and paddle the gentle waters past Roosevelt Island, the Kennedy Center, the Lincoln Memorial, and the Georgetown Waterfront Park.

12
Oak Hill Cemetery

📍 D3 🏛 3001 R St, NW Ⓜ Dupont Circle, then bus 🕐 9am–4:30pm Mon–Fri, 11am–4pm Sat, 1–4pm Sun 🎫 Federal hols 🌐 oakhill cemeterydc.org

Washingtonian banker, art collector, and philanthropist William Wilson Corcoran bought the land on which Congress established the Oak Hill Cemetery in 1849. Today, about 18,000 graves cover this 25-acre (10-ha) site, which is planted with huge oak trees. Members of some of the city's most prominent families are buried here, their names featured throughout its history,

↓ The imposing facade of Georgetown University

↑ Georgetown Waterfront Park, a peaceful spot to take a break

including Magruder, Thomas, Beall, and Marbury. Lincoln's son William is also buried here.

At the cemetery's entrance is an Italianate gatehouse that is still used as the superintendent's lodge and office. Northeast of it is the Spencer family monument, designed by Louis Comfort Tiffany. The granite low-relief of an angel is signed by Tiffany.

Another notable monument is the Van Ness mausoleum, built in 1833 for the wife of John Peter Van Ness, mayor of Washington, DC. Designed by George Hadfield, it is said to be a copy of the Temple of Vesta in Rome.

Also worth visiting is the Gothic chapel designed by James Renwick and located on the cemetery's highest ridge, near the intersection of 29th and R streets, NW. Nearby is the grave of John Howard Payne, composer of the well-loved song "Home, Sweet Home," who died in 1852. The bust atop Payne's monument was originally sculpted with a full beard, but Corcoran asked a stonemason to "shave the statue" and it now appears clean-shaven.

13

Georgetown Waterfront Park

📍 C5 🚪 Bottom of Wisconsin Ave Ⓜ Foggy Bottom-GWU, then 15 min walk 🌐 georgetown waterfrontpark.org

This lovely riverfront park adjacent to Washington Harbour offers locals and visitors alike a place to enjoy the surprising beauty of the Potomac River. Shaded lawns offer respite in summer, and inviting benches offer wonderful views of the park and river. There is also a great view downriver to the Kennedy Center. Wide walking paths extend north to Georgetown and south to East Potomac Park along the popular Capital Crescent Trail. Overlooks along the riverfront are decorated with carved panels that tell the story of the area's early days as a busy port. There is also a labyrinth that is popular with kids and those seeking serenity. A stream gauge at the western end of the park lets visitors check the height of the river water.

14

Mount Zion Church

📍 D4 🚪 1334 29th St, NW Ⓜ Foggy Bottom-GWU, Dupont Circle, then bus 🌐 mtzionumcdc.org

This church is thought to have had the first Black congregation in DC. The original church, at 27th and P streets, was a "station" on the city's original Underground Railroad, offering shelter for enslaved people on their journey north to freedom. The present redbrick building was completed in 1884 after the first church burned down. Mount Zion Cemetery, the oldest Black burial ground in the city, is nearby, in the middle of the 2500 block of Q Street.

STAY

Georgetown Inn
In the heart of Georgetown, this classic boutique hotel is near trendy shops, pubs, and restaurants.

📍 C4 🚪 1310 Wisconsin Ave, NW 🌐 georgetowninn.com

$ $ $

> **The bust atop Payne's monument was originally sculpted with a full beard, but Corcoran asked a stonemason to "shave the statue" and it now appears clean shaven.**

A LONG WALK
GEORGETOWN

Distance 5 km (3 miles) **Time** 60 minutes
Nearest Metro Foggy Bottom

Renowned for its beautiful and historic architecture, eclectic shops, and delightful restaurants, Georgetown has it all. Starting in upper Georgetown, this walk takes you along residential streets past grand homes and Federal-style rowhouses, past early churches and cemeteries, parks and river vistas, quiet lanes, and crowded streets. The walk ends at Washington Harbour, passing through the commercial heart of Georgetown. Details of many sights mentioned are in the section on Georgetown (*p119*).

Start the walk at **Dumbarton Oaks** *(p125), a Federal-style mansion containing a huge collection of pre-Columbian and Byzantine art.*

START Dumbarton Oaks

Admire **Tudor Place**, *designed by the Capitol architect William Thornton.*

Georgetown University *(p124), founded in 1789. Former US president Bill Clinton was a graduate here.*

Number 3307 at Smith Row, *home to John and Jackie Kennedy between 1957 and 1961.*

Cady's Alley *(p127) with its high-end home furnishing shops.*

Francis Scott Key Memorial

The **Francis Scott Key Bridge** *and the* **Francis Scott Key Memorial** *(p127), named after the author of "The Star-Spangled Banner."*

Francis Scott Key Memorial Bridge

Martin's Tavern *(p125) has served every president from Truman onward. It was here that Senator John F. Kennedy proposed to Jacqueline Lee Bouvier in 1953.*

St. John's Episcopal Church

Smith Row

Martin's Tavern

Grace Church

Georgetown Waterfront Park

↑ Colorful houses lining the charming Chesapeake and Ohio Canal

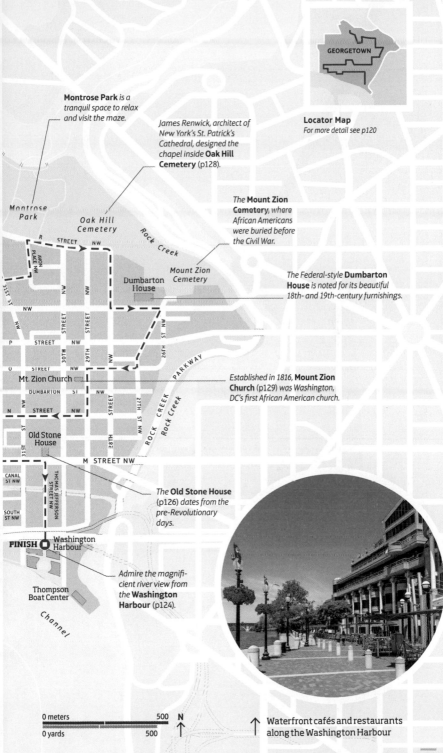

Montrose Park *is a tranquil space to relax and visit the maze.*

James Renwick, architect of New York's St. Patrick's Cathedral, designed the chapel inside **Oak Hill Cemetery** *(p128).*

(p128)

The **Mount Zion Cemetery***, where African Americans were buried before the Civil War.*

Montrose Park

Oak Hill Cemetery

Rock Creek

R STREET NW

AVON PLACE NW

31ST ST

Mount Zion Cemetery

Dumbarton House

The Federal-style **Dumbarton House** *is noted for its beautiful 18th- and 19th-century furnishings.*

STREET NW

STREET NW

NW

NW

26TH ST NW

P STREET NW

30TH ST NW

29TH ST NW

ROCK CREEK PARKWAY

O STREET NW

Mt. Zion Church

DUMBARTON ST NW

27TH ST NW

Rock Creek

Established in 1816, **Mount Zion Church** *(p129) was Washington, DC's first African American church.*

(p129)

N STREET NW

Old Stone House

31ST ST

28TH ST

Rock Creek

M STREET NW

CANAL ST NW

THOMAS JEFFERSON STREET NW

SOUTH ST NW

The **Old Stone House** *(p126) dates from the pre-Revolutionary days.*

(p126)

FINISH Washington Harbour

Thompson Boat Center

Channel

Admire the magnificient river view from the **Washington Harbour** *(p124).*

(p124)

Locator Map
For more detail see p120

GEORGETOWN

| 0 meters | 500 |
| 0 yards | 500 |

N

↑ Waterfront cafés and restaurants along the Washington Harbour

SOUTH OF THE NATIONAL MALL

A decade ago, this part of the city was made up of aging warehouses, government buildings, and third-rate office complexes that were a wasteland for visitors. A radical multibillion-dollar makeover has transformed the area into a shiny riverfront playground for dining, shopping, and entertainment in the city. Cornerstones of the region are the Nationals Park and the phenomenal District Wharf development, a mile-long (1.5-km) stretch of gleaming glass and steel high-rises offering some of DC's hottest new restaurants, waterfront parks, live music venues, and several ways to get out on the river for a good time. There is one thing that did not change, except for the better: the old fish market where traditional, open-air, family-run stalls and restaurants offer superfresh seafood raw or cooked to order.

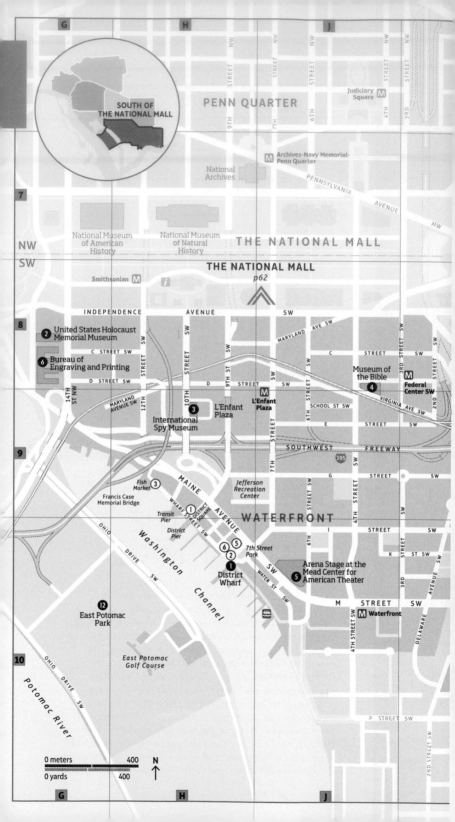

SOUTH OF THE NATIONAL MALL

Must Sees

1. District Wharf
2. United States Holocaust Memorial Museum
3. International Spy Museum

Experience More

4. Museum of the Bible
5. Arena Stage at the Mead Center for American Theater
6. Bureau of Engraving and Printing
7. Yards Park
8. Nationals Park
9. National Museum of the US Navy
10. Cold War Gallery
11. Culture House DC
12. East Potomac Park
13. Barrack's Row

Eat

1. Mi Vida
2. Hank's Oyster Bar
3. Jessie Taylor Seafood
4. Rose's Luxury

Drink

5. Bluejacket

Stay

6. Canopy by Hilton
7. Hyatt House Washington DC/ The Wharf

Did You Know?

The Wharf Jitney offers a free ride across the Washington Channel to East Potomac Park.

❶ DISTRICT WHARF

📍 **H10** 🚇 **Maine Ave, SW between Market Sq & 7th St, SW** Ⓜ **Waterfront, L'Enfant Plaza** 🚌 **52, 74** 🕐 **Daily** 🌐 **wharfdc.com**

This neighborhood was filled with crumbling government and office buildings and military warehouses only a few years ago. Today, an expensive facelift has resulted in this exciting waterside development along Washington Channel.

On the waterfront, the largest pier is home to the traditional Maine Avenue Fish Market, where you can select and take home ultrafresh seafood, or have it cooked to order to eat onsite. Other piers include Transit Pier, where live concerts take place and water taxis ply their trade, and District Pier, dedicated to a wide range of entertainment and recreation. Several park-like open areas offer shaded spots to sit and enjoy great views of the bustling marinas, and there are enough inviting restaurants and trendy shops to keep visitors entertained for hours. Pop into A Beautiful Closet for home decor and gifts, the Martha Spak Gallery for fine contemporary art from local artists, or the Politics and Prose bookstore for an excellent book selection and lots of author readings. Take a break at Mi Vida for Mexican food, Kaliwa for Southeast Asian seafood, Del Mar de Fabio Trabocchi for Spanish-style seafood, and Hank's Oyster Bar for seafood.

📷 PICTURE PERFECT
Potomac Pictures

The water taxi running between Washington Harbour, Georgetown, and National Harbor provides splendid photo opportunities. Try to catch it around sunset for the best pictures of the city skyline and the Potomac River.

EAT

Mi Vida
Mexican street food and
an avant-garde take on
home cooking.

⦿H9 ⌂98 District Sq, SW
Ⓦmividamexico.com

$$$

Hank's Oyster Bar
Enjoy fresh New
England-style seafood.

⦿H10 ⌂701 Wharf St,
SW Ⓦhanksoyster
bar.com

$$$

Jessie Taylor Seafood
Freshly cooked seafood
beside the Wharf.

⦿H9 ⌂1100 Maine Ave
Ⓦjessietaylor
seafood.com

$$$

↑ Washington's gleaming
waterfront develop-
ment at District Wharf

1 Opened in 1805, the Maine
Avenue Fish Market is one of
the country's oldest contin-
ually operating fish markets,
with stalwarts such as Jessie
Taylor Seafood.

2 Seafood dishes are a popular
choice at District Wharf.

3 Waterfront Park offers
visitors lovely views of the
busy marinas, the Washington
Channel, and the serene
Potomac River.

6,000,000
—
Jews and millions of others were killed by the Nazi government as part of the "Final Solution."

↑ The three-story "Tower of Faces," devoted to the Jewish community of Eišiškės, Lithuania

UNITED STATES HOLOCAUST MEMORIAL MUSEUM

G0 **100 Raoul Wallenburg Place, SW** **M Smithsonian** **13 (Pentagon shuttle)** **10am-5:30pm daily** **Yom Kippur, Dec 25** **ushmm.org**

Solemn and respectful yet engrossing and informative, the challenging Holocaust Museum is a study center for issues relating to the Holocaust as well as a national memorial for the millions murdered by the Nazi government during World War II.

The museum, opened in 1993, bears witness to the systematic persecution and murder in Europe of millions of Jews and others deemed undesirable by the Third Reich, including political objectors, intellectuals, Sinti and Roma peoples, homosexuals, and people with disabilities. The space ranges from the intentionally claustrophobic to the soaringly majestic. About 2,500 photographs, 1,000 artifacts, 53 video monitors, and 30 interactive stations containing graphic and emotionally disturbing images of violence grimly detail the surveillance and loss of individual rights, forcing visitors to confront the horror of the Holocaust. While "Daniel's Story" is aimed at children of eight years and up, the permanent exhibition is not recommended for those under 12 years. Free timed passes are needed from March to August; same-day walk-up passes are available alongside online advance and same-day passes.

↑ The museum building, designed to reference Holocaust sites via its abstract architectural forms

GALLERY GUIDE

The Holocaust Museum is meant to be an immersive experience. Starting from the top, footage, artifacts, photographs, and survivor testimonies can be seen from the fourth to the second floors. The first floor has the Hall of Witness and "Daniel's Story," and the Concourse has the Children's Tile Wall.

↑ The "Final Solution" exhibit, including a boxcar used to carry prisoners to concentration camps

③ ✍ M □ 🗄

INTERNATIONAL SPY MUSEUM

📍H9 🏠700 L'Enfant Plaza, SW Ⓜ L'Enfant Plaza 🕐Times vary, check website 🚫Jan 1, Thanksgiving, Dec 25 🌐spymuseum.org

This fascinating museum shows the world of spycraft and how intelligence gathering and espionage shape the world we live in. The one-of-a-kind, world-class collection of spy gadgets and memorabilia enhances the fascinating museum experience, which assumes that each guest is a spy in training.

Becoming an effective spy requires many skills and tools, and "School for Spies" not only explains them but also provides insights into how and why people become spies. "Spies Among Us" has stories of real-life spies and interactive codebreaking exhibits. The celebrity spies exhibit includes actress Marlene Dietrich and director John Ford, while "The Secret History of History" tells tales of espionage from biblical times to the early 20th century. Visitors' newfound skills can be put into practice by joining the immersive "Operation Spy" program. In 2019, the museum relocated to L'Enfant Plaza at the hub of the rapidly upscaling Southwest DC area, where expansive new facilities include a lecture theater and a vast rooftop terrace. An underground mall here has eateries with affordable food, and an outdoor entertainment area that hosts free summer concerts.

↑ The Cyber Command, an interactive exhibit at the museum

→ Sculpture from the Spying that Shaped History exhibit

Timeline

c 1800 BC
△ A clay tablet from Dabylonian king Hammurabi records information about his spies – the oldest record of espionage.

1778
△ Benjamin Franklin becomes the United States ambassador to France; in fact, he is one of the country's earliest spies.

1950–80
△ The Cold War triggers a renaissance in spy-craft, with microdot cameras creating images the size of a newspaper punctuation mark.

2018
△ Modern tech turns everyone into a spy: tiny drones built using standard electronics can eavesdrop on cell phone conversations.

Did You Know?

George Washington's spy code name was 711 and Congress paid him $17,000 for espionage expenses.

↑ Exterior of the International Spy Museum at L'Enfant Plaza

One of the immersive
exhibits at the massive
Museum of the Bible ↑

EXPERIENCE MORE

4 Ⓜ Ⓟ 🛍
Museum of the Bible

📍 J8 🏛 400 4th St,
SW Ⓜ L'Enfant Plaza
🕐 10am–5pm daily 🚫 Jan 1,
Thanksgiving, Dec 25
🌐 museumofthebible.org

Containing what may well be
the world's largest collection of
Bibles and biblical artifacts, the
Museum of the Bible is one of
Washington's major attractions.
It fills six floors of a large build-
ing that was the 1923 Terminal
Refrigerating and Warehousing
Company before it had an esti-
mated $400 million makeover.

The aim of the museum is
to document the history and
impact of the Bible, as well
as relate the stories within
it. The first floor features a
collection of art and printed
works from the Vatican
museums. The second floor
traces the impact of the Bible
from ancient to modern times.
The third floor focuses on
relating the stories of the
Hebrew Bible and Nazareth
in the era of Jesus. The fourth

floor relates the history of the
Bible, and the fifth floor has a
remarkable collection of antiquities from ancient Israel. On
the mezzanine is Milk + Honey
Café, which serves coffee and
snacks, while on the sixth floor
is the atrium. It offers one of
the most breathtaking views
of Washington, DC.

5 💻 🛍
Arena Stage at the Mead Center for American Theater

📍 J10 🏛 1101 6th St SW
Ⓜ Waterfront 🌐 arena
stage.org

Founded in 1950, the Arena
Stage was one of the first
nonprofit theaters in the US,
and is dedicated to promoting
American plays and play-
wrights. The award-winning
theater has a long history of
producing not only classic
works, but new, cutting-edge
works by emerging writers.
In 1967 the arena became
the first regional theater to

produce a play that went on to
Broadway – Howard Sackler's
The Great White Hope, which
won the best play Tony in 1969.

6 Ⓜ 🛍
Bureau of Engraving and Printing

📍 G8 🏛 14th & C Sts, SW
Ⓜ Smithsonian 🕐 For
tours: times vary, check
website 🚫 Week after
Christmas, Federal hols
🌐 moneyfactory.gov

Until 1863, individual banks
were responsible for printing

💬 INSIDER TIP
Water Taxis

Water taxis run by the
Potomac Riverboat
Company *(potomacriver
boatco.com)* from Old
Town Alexandria, the
National Harbor, and
Georgetown to the
Wharf offer spectacular
views of the Potomac.

American money. A shortage of coins and the need to finance the Civil War led to the production of standardized banknotes, and the Bureau of Engraving and Printing was founded. Initially housed in the Treasury Building (p112), it was moved to its present location in 1914. It prints over $140 billion a year, as well as stamps, Federal documents, and White House invitations. The 40-minute tour includes a short film, and a walk through the building to view the printing processes. Also on display are bills that are out of circulation, counterfeit money, and a special $100,000 bill.

Yards Park

📍 L10 🏠 355 Water St, SE
Ⓜ Navy Yard-Ballpark
🌐 capitolriverfront.org/yards-park

This lovely, expansive public space that stretches along the banks of the Anacostia River is quickly becoming a favorite with DC residents. The centerpiece of this family-oriented park is a large wading pool that children and adults are encouraged to splash around in. The dancing fountains are a water art feature that visitors can run through – a very popular attraction on hot summer days. Green lawns make a great place for picnics, and there are tree-shaded benches and a pleasant waterfront walkway. Buildings surrounding the park house an array of fine and fast-food restaurants. Free movies and concerts are put on during the summer, and the park plays host to the DC Jazz Festival.

EAT & DRINK

Rose's Luxury

This Barracks Row favorite offers delicious New American daily menus (a choice of two dishes and dessert).

📍 M9 🏠 717 8th St, SE
🌐 rosesluxury.com

💲💲💲

Bluejacket

Popular microbrewery, restaurant and bar in a century-old former munitions factory. Nationals fans flock here before and after games.

📍 P4 🏠 300 Tingey St, SE 🌐 bluejacketdc.com

💲💲

↓ A cooling water feature at the leafy Yards Park

STAY

Canopy by Hilton
This nautical-themed boutique hotel with a rooftop bar and river views offers evening tastings of local wines, brews, or spirits.

📍H10 🏠975 7th St, SW 🌐hilton.com/en/canopy

💲💲💲

Hyatt House Washington DC/ The Wharf
Extended-stay hotel with expansive river views. Some rooms have a kitchenette and living area. There's also a fitness room, seasonal outdoor swimming pool, and complimentary breakfast.

📍H10 🏠725 Wharf St, SW 🌐hyatt.com

💲💲💲

Nationals Park

📍L10 🏠1500 S Capitol St, SE Ⓜ Navy Yard-Ballpark, Capitol South 🌐mlb.com/nationals/ballpark

Another popular venue at the expanding Southwest Waterfront, the $784 million Nationals Park was opened in 2008. President George W. Bush threw the ceremonial first pitch. The stadium has a seating capacity of 41,339, as well as 79 suites on three levels, and is the first LEED-certified green major league stadium in the US. From the upper stands visitors can take in a view stretching to the Washington Monument and the US Capitol. In honor of the Naval Yards in the surrounding area, since 2011 the stadium has sounded a submarine "dive" klaxon when the Nationals baseball team scores a home run.

National Museum of the US Navy

📍M10 🏠736 Sicard St, SE, Building 76 Ⓜ Navy Yard-Ballpark, Eastern Market 🕐9am–4pm Mon-Sat (from 10am Sat); valid US navy or military photo ID or advance permission needed, see website 🌐history.navy.mil/nmusn

This museum contains exhibits tracing the history of the US Navy from the Revolutionary War to modern times. Themes include the role of the navy in the Civil War, the shift from wood to steel, and the rise of the Great White Fleet, among others. A large exhibit focuses on deep-sea exploration and features the bathyscaphe (manned submersible) *Trieste*, which made a record dive to 35,797 ft (10,910 m) in the Mariana Trench in 1960. The exhibit also features a full-size replica of the deep sea submersible *Alvin* (DSV-2). The exhibit "The Forgotten Wars of the 19th Century" displays a replica of the gun deck of the famous USS *Constitution*, the wooden-hulled, three-masted frigate named by George Washington after the

Constitution of the new United States and affectionately known as Old Ironsides.

Cold War Gallery

📍M10 🏠736 Sicard St, SE, Building 70 Ⓜ Navy Yard-Ballpark, Eastern Market 🕐Times vary, check website; valid US Department of Defense photo ID or advance permission needed, see website 🌐history.navy.mil/nmusn

Located next door to the Navy Museum, this large museum defines the Cold War and tells the story of the US Navy's role in fighting it. One of the first exhibits visitors experience is the "Ready Room," a reproduction of a real ready room, where pilots would get their

← Nautical exhibits on display at the National Museum of the US Navy

3,020

cherry trees were gifted to the city by Japan in 1912 and planted in this area by 1920.

↑ Exquisite cherry trees in full bloom along the waterfront of East Potomac Park

orders just before flying out to undertake top secret missions. Other exhibits in the museum cover the role the United States played in the Korean and Vietnam wars, nuclear-era technology, and the gathering of intelligence with submarines, high-altitude aircraft, and satellites. The "Covert Submarine Operations" exhibit has on display a full nuclear submarine command center from the USS *Trepang*, a Sturgeon-class attack submarine that was in service from 1970 to 1999.

11

Culture House DC

🚩 K9 🏠 700 Delaware Ave, SW Ⓜ Waterfront ⏰ Times vary, check website 🌐 culturehousedc.org

It is hard not to fall in love at first sight with this dazzlingly painted 1886 Baptist church, now a fascinating center for the presentation and promotion of art. It has a 15,000-sq-ft (1,394-m) mural-covered interior, created as a public gathering and performance space. The center is dedicated to providing a dynamic environment for concerts and performances of all types, and where people of all ages can celebrate and create art. The Art Annex, a gallery open to the public on weekends, hosts shows of regionally and nationally known artists. Outside, there are organic gardens that create produce for local shops and restaurants.

12

East Potomac Park

🚩 H10 🏠 Ohio Dr, SW Ⓜ Waterfront

This low-key park occupies a long peninsula that extends south of the Tidal Basin and separates the Washington Channel from the Potomac River. A leafy green expanse, with a loop road and broad lawns, it is favored by joggers, cyclists, and anyone who wants to experience a quieter spot along the riverfront.

13

Barracks Row

🚩 M9 🏠 8th St, SE (between D & I streets) Ⓜ Eastern Market 🌐 barracksrow.org

The stretch of 8th Street between D and I streets is known as Barracks Row, the oldest commercial district in the city and scene of a major renaissance since about 2010. The strip takes its name from the Marine Barracks established here in 1801, but today it is best known as an up-and-coming restaurant and shopping destination. Highlights include Jeni's Splendid Ice Creams and District Doughnut.

NORTHWEST

A remarkable area with two distinctly different personalities, the Northwest is a collection of old and new neighborhoods. Kalorama, lying northwest of L'Enfant's original city limits, remained a mainly rural area until the end of the 19th century, when Congress ordered the city plan to be extended outward. Today, Kalorama and Embassy Row are highly walkable areas, with lovely tree-shaded sidewalks and a century's worth of elegant mansions lining the streets, many containing embassies from around the world. Dupont Circle and the multicultural Adams-Morgan are the area's established cool neighborhoods where you will find bookstores, wine shops, restaurants, and nightlife. Farther east, the culturally rich and varied Shaw neighborhood had its origins in settlements set up in the city's rural outskirts by newly freed enslaved people coming to the north. Shaw's famous U Street corridor is now one of the city's trendiest zones, with cutting-edge restaurants vying for space with gastropubs and mezcal bars. Here, too, are the historic Howard and Lincoln theaters, once famous stages in the "Black Broadway." Now renovated, they present a full schedule of plays and concerts with a strong theme of diversity.

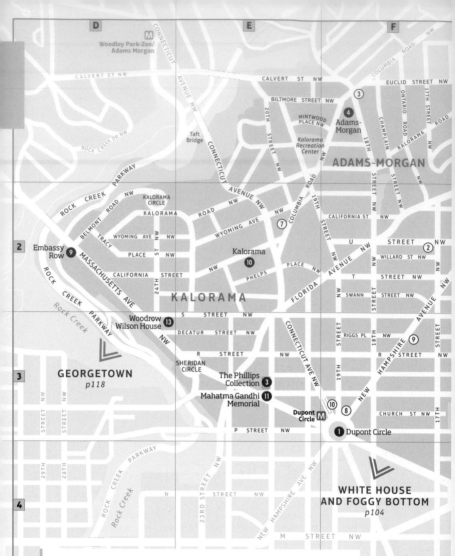

NORTHWEST

Experience
1 Dupont Circle
2 Meridian Hill Park
3 The Phillips Collection
4 Adams-Morgan
5 Howard University
6 14th and U Streets, NW
7 Mary McLeod Bethune Council House National Historic Site
8 African American Civil War Memorial and Museum
9 Embassy Row
10 Kalorama
11 Mahatma Gandhi Memorial
12 Lincoln Theatre
13 Woodrow Wilson House

Eat & Drink
1 Ben's Chili Bowl
2 Henry's Soul Café
3 Madam's Organ
4 Busboys and Poets
5 Convivial
6 Right Proper Brewing

Stay
7 American Guest House
8 The Dupont Circle Hotel
9 Lyle Washington DC

Shop
10 Kramerbooks & Afterwords Café

EXPERIENCE

① 🍴 🥤 🛍️

Dupont Circle

📍F3 Ⓜ️Dupont Circle

This area to the north of the White House gets its name from the park-like Dupont traffic circle and the lovely Francis Dupont Memorial Fountain, named for a naval Civil War hero. In the early 20th century the Dupont Circle area was a place of grand mansions, but over the years its fortunes declined. Then, in the 1970s, Washingtonians began to buy and restore the decaying old buildings. The district is now one of the liveliest and most sophisticated in DC, with art galleries, bars, restaurants, and bookstores. The present marble fountain, constructed

in 1921, has four figures – representing the sea, the wind, the stars, and the navigational arts – supporting a marble basin. The park around the fountain draws a cross section of the community – chess players engrossed in their games, cyclists pausing at the fountain, picnickers, and tourists taking a break.

②

Meridian Hill Park

📍G1 🏛️16th & W Sts, NW Ⓜ️U Street/African Amer Civil War Memorial/Cardozo 🌐nps.gov/places/meridian-hill-park.htm

In 1819, John Porter built an ornate mansion on Meridian Hill, so named because it was on the exact longitude of the original DC milestone marker set in April 1791. The mansion was later the home of outgoing president John Quincy Adams. Just before the Civil War, a pleasure park was developed on the hill, which later became a bivouac area for Union soldiers during the war. Begun in 1914, the ornate,

Italianate-style park of today has spreading shade trees, grassy expanses, wide stone stairways, and hilltop terraces with views across the park. The centerpiece is a spectacular fountain that cascades down the hillside through 13 basins. The park's Joan of Arc statue is the city's only equestrian statue of a woman. The popular park can get busy, especially in summer when the grounds are occupied by families enjoying picnics.

③ 🎨 🎵 🥤 🛍️

The Phillips Collection

📍E3 🏛️1600 21st St at Q St, NW Ⓜ️Dupont Circle 🕐10am–5pm Tue–Sat (to 8:30pm Thu), 11am–6pm Sun 🚫Jan 1, Jul 4, Thanksgiving, Dec 25, Federal hols 🌐phillips collection.org

This is one of the world's finest collections of Impressionist and contemporary art, and the first museum devoted to modern art in the US. It was founded in 1917 by Duncan and Marjorie Phillips, who opened part of their home as the Phillips Memorial Gallery.

The couple spent their time traveling and adding to their already extensive collection. During the 1920s they acquired some of the most important modern European paintings, including *The Luncheon of the Boating Party* (1881) by Renoir.

Their elegant 1897 Georgian-Revival home is now the permanent gallery for the Phillips Collection, and provides an intimate space for appreciating the artworks. The collection has over 43,000

← The Francis Dupont Memorial Fountain at Dupont Circle

↑ Colorful restaurants, cafés, and stores in the vibrant Adams-Morgan neighborhood

pieces of 19th, 20th, and 21st-century American and European art. There is a wonderful group of Impressionist and Post-Impressionist works: *Dancers at the Barre* by Degas, *Self-Portrait* by Cézanne, and *Entrance to the Public Gardens in Arles* by Van Gogh are just three examples. The museum has one of the world's largest collections of works by French artist Pierre Bonnard, including *The Open Window* (1921), plus several large Rothko pieces.

On the first Thursday of each month the museum hosts "Phillips after 5," evenings of gallery talks and live music. On Sunday afternoons from September through May, a series of concerts is staged in the gallery's Music Room.

attracted by the district's lively streets and its colorful, early 20th-century houses and apartments. The area has a thriving music and nightlife scene that buzzes into the early morning hours. A wide variety of world cuisines can be found in the restaurants along 18th Street and Columbia Road. This cultural diversity is celebrated in September each year with food, music, and dance at the Adams-Morgan Day Festival.

④ 🍴 🖥 🏛

Adams-Morgan

📍 **F1** 🏛 North of Dupont Circle, east of Rock Creek Park, and south of Mount Pleasant Ⓜ Dupont Circle, Woodley Park-Zoo/Adams Morgan

Packed with cafés, bookstores, clubs, and galleries, Adams-Morgan was one of the city's first racially diverse neighborhoods and is a vibrant mix of LGBTQ+ and straight African, Hispanic, and Caribbean immigrants. People are

EAT & DRINK

Ben's Chili Bowl
Legendary 1950s-style diner serving all the city's movers and shakers.

📍 **H2** 🏛 1213 U St, NW
🌐 benschilibowl.com

💲💲💲

Henry's Soul Café
This diner has been serving tasty Southern classics since 1968.

📍 **F2** 🏛 1704 U St, NW
🌐 henryssoulcafe.com

💲💲💲

Madam's Organ
Live music nightly at this popular blues bar and soul food restaurant.

📍 **F1** 🏛 2461 18th St, NW
🌐 madamsorgan.com

💲💲💲

Busboys and Poets
Excellent vegetarian, vegan, and meat entrees served 24 hours daily.

📍 **G2** 🏛 2021 14th St, NW
🌐 busboysandpoets.com

💲💲💲

Convivial
Indulgent, perfectly executed French American fare and craft cocktails.

📍 **F2** 🏛 801 O St, NW
🌐 convivialdc.com

💲💲💲

Right Proper Brewing
Brewpub with local beers and casual Southern comfort food from the kitchen.

📍 **J2** 🏛 624 T St, NW
🕐 D only Mon-Thu
🌐 rightproperbrewing.com

💲💲💲

The intersection of 14th and U streets, one of the liveliest districts in the city ↑

5
Howard University

J2 **2400 6th St, NW** **Shaw-Howard University** **howard.edu**

The first Congregational Society of Washington, DC set up a seminary in 1866 for the education of African Americans. The concept expanded to include a university, and within two years the Colleges of Liberal Arts and Medicine of Howard University were founded, named for General Oliver O. Howard (1830–1909), an abolitionist and Civil War general.

Famous graduates include Thurgood Marshall, the first African American Supreme Court Justice, historian Carter Woodson, writers Ta-Nehisi Coates and Toni Morrison, actor and writer Ossie Davis, civil rights activist Stokely Carmichael, and rapper and music mogul Sean Combs, better known as Puff Daddy.

The university's art gallery displays works by African and American artists, including Henry O. Tanner and Edmonia Lewis. Other highlights include the Gothic-style Andrew Rankin Memorial Chapel, Frederick Douglass Memorial Hall, and the monumental Founder's Library.

6
14th and U Streets, NW

G2 **U Street/African Amer Civil War Memorial/ Cardozo**

The intersection of 14th and U streets, NW is the gateway to one of Washington's most vibrant neighborhoods. Until the mid-20th century, U Street, once known as the "Black Broadway," hosted prominent African American entertainers, including Duke Ellington and Pearl Bailey. They performed at the Lincoln and Howard theaters as well as in many nightclubs. 14th Street, known as Automobile Row, was lined with posh car showrooms. But in 1968 both 14th and U streets burned in the riots that ensued after the assassination of Dr. Martin Luther King. Businesses fled the area and for decades it was left to drug trafficking and crime. The well-respected local Studio Theatre bought a derelict car showroom in 1997 and built a state-of-the-art performance space. High-end apartments, restaurants, independent boutiques, music venues, and bars followed. Today, the area, known as the U Street Corridor, is a thriving

THE SHAW NEIGHBORHOOD

This neighborhood is named for Union Colonel Robert Gould Shaw, the white commander of an all-Black regiment from Massachusetts. He supported his men in their struggle to attain the same rights as white soldiers. Until the 1960s, U Street was home to flourishing African American businesses and organizations. Thriving theaters, such as the Howard and the Lincoln, attracted top-name artists, and Howard University was the center of intellectual life for Black students. The 1968 riots, sparked by the assassination of Dr. Martin Luther King, Jr., wiped out much of Shaw's business district, and many thought the area could never be revived. However, the restoration of the Lincoln, the renewal of the business district, and an influx of buyers renovating historic houses have all contributed to the rejuvenation, with trendy bars, clubs, and stores opening on U Street.

spot for dining, shopping, and entertainment. Of note is the famous Ben's Chili Bowl *(p151)*, established in 1950.

7

Mary McLeod Bethune Council House National Historic Site

◊ G4 **⌂ 1318 Vermont Ave, NW** **Ⓜ McPherson Square, Mt Vernon Sq/7th St-Convention Center** **◷ 9am-5pm Thu-Sat** **⚑ Jan 1, Thanksgiving, Dec 25** **ⓦ nps.gov/mamc**

Born in 1875 to parents formerly enslaved, Mary McLeod Bethune was an educator and civil and women's rights activist. In 1904 she founded the Daytona Literary and Industrial School for Negro Girls, a college for impoverished Black women in Florida. Renamed the Bethune-Cookman College in 1931, it achieved university status in 2007.

In the 1930s, Franklin D. Roosevelt asked Bethune to be his special advisor on racial affairs, and she later became director of the Division of Negro Affairs in the National Youth Administration. As part of President Roosevelt's cabinet, she was the first Black woman to obtain a high position in the US government.

Bethune went on to found the National Council of Negro Women, which gives voice to the concerns of Black women. It grew to have a membership of 10,000, and this house was bought by Bethune and the council as its headquarters. It was not until November 1979, 24 years after Bethune's death, that the house was opened to the public, with photographs, manuscripts, and other artifacts from her life on display. In 1982 the house was declared a National Historic Site and was bought by the National Park Service.

8 Ⓜ 🏛

African American Civil War Memorial and Museum

◊ H2 **⌂ Museum: 1925 Vermont Ave, NW; memorial: 10th & U Sts, NW** **Ⓜ U Street/African Amer Civil War Memorial/Cardozo** **◷ 10am-5pm Mon, 10am-6:30pm Tue-Fri, 10am-4pm Sat, noon-4pm Sun** **ⓦ afroamcivilwar.org**

Opened in January 1999, the African American Civil War Museum uses photographs, documents, and audiovisual equipment to tell the story of the soldiers who fought for freedom from slavery during the Civil War. The museum's permanent exhibition is entitled "Slavery to Freedom: Civil War to Civil Rights." Interactive kiosks bring together historic documents, photographs, and music in a powerful and evocative way. There is also a service for anyone interested in tracing relatives who may have served with United States Colored Troops during the Civil War.

At the center of a paved plaza nearby is the *Spirit of Freedom*, a sculpture by Ed Hamilton, which was unveiled on July 18, 1998. It is the first major art piece by a Black sculptor on Federal land in the District of Columbia. Standing 10 ft (3 m) tall, the memorial features Black soldiers and a sailor poised to leave home.

STAY

American Guest House

Classic 1898 row house B&B in Kalorama. Its 12 guest rooms, elegantly furnished with antiques, have modern amenities. A lavish breakfast is included.

◊ E2 **⌂ 2005 Columbia Rd, NW** **ⓦ americanguest house.com**

$$$ ⓢⓢⓢ

The Dupont Circle Hotel

Located on Dupont Circle with easy access to vibrant nightlife and hip restaurants. The guest rooms are modern, and some suites have balconies with city views.

◊ F3 **⌂ 1500 New Hampshire Ave, NW** **ⓦ doylecollection.com/hotels/the-dupont-circle-hotel**

ⓢⓢⓢ

Lyle Washington DC

Boutique hotel with Art Deco styling just three blocks from Dupont Circle. The in-house restaurant, Lyle's, offers fine dining.

◊ F3 **⌂ 1731 New Hampshire Ave, NW** **ⓦ lyledc.com**

ⓢⓢⓢ

← Ed Hamilton's *Spirit of Freedom* sculpture at the African American Civil War Memorial

← The Greek Embassy on Embassy Row, Kalorama

apartment buildings are on Connecticut Avenue, south of the Taft Bridge that crosses Rock Creek Park. Most notable are the Georgian Revival-style apartments at number 2126, the Beaux Arts-inspired building at 1914, and the Spanish Colonial-style apartments at 2311. Also worth a look is the Tudor-style building at 2221 Kalorama Road.

⑨ Embassy Row

📍D2 🏛Massachusetts Ave, NW Ⓜ Dupont Circle

Stretching from Scott Circle toward Observatory Circle, Embassy Row developed during the Depression when many of the city's wealthy families were forced to sell their mansions to diplomats, who bought them for foreign missions. Since then, many more embassies have been built, often in the vernacular style of their native country, making the row architecturally fascinating. At number 2315 Massachusetts Avenue, the former Embassy of Pakistan, is an opulent 1908 mansion with a mansard roof and a rounded wall that hugs the corner. At 2349 is the 1905 Embassy of the Republic of Cameroon, one of the avenue's great early 20th-century Beaux Arts masterpieces. Opposite the embassy stands a statue of

> 🏔 **GREAT VIEW**
> **Rock Creek Park**
>
> The best views of the stunning expanse of nearby Rock Creek Park (p171) are from Kalorama Circle at the northern end of 24th Street.

the Irish revolutionary Robert Emmet (1778–1803), commissioned by Irish Americans to commemorate Irish independence (the Irish Embassy is further down at number 2234). At 2536 is the Embassy of India. Two carved elephants stand outside as symbols of Indian culture and mythology. The British Embassy at 3100 was designed by Edwin Lutyens in 1928. Outside is an arresting statue of Winston Churchill by William M. McVey.

⑩ Kalorama

📍E2 Ⓜ Woodley Park-Zoo/Adams Morgan, Dupont Circle

A district of stately private homes and elegant apartment buildings, Kalorama (Greek for "beautiful view") has been home to the wealthy since its development at the turn of the 20th century as a suburb. Five presidents had homes here: Herbert Hoover, Franklin D. Roosevelt, Warren Harding, William Taft, and Woodrow Wilson. Some of the city's most striking and ornate

⑪ Mahatma Gandhi Memorial

📍E3 🏛2100-2120 Q St, NW, across the street from the Embassy of India Ⓜ Dupont Circle

In the park in front of the Indian Embassy stands a bronze statue of Mahatma

→ The striking Mahatma Gandhi Memorial statue

Gandhi by Indian sculptor Gautam Pal. Born Mohandas Karamchand Gandhi, the Mahatma became famous around the world for his ideas of ahimsa and nonviolent protest against the colonial rule of Britain over India. In his later years he lived an ascetic's life, and the statue depicts him in simple garb during his 1930 Dandi March protesting against the British-imposed salt tax. Inscribed on the statue is Gandhi's philosophy: "My life is my message."

12

Lincoln Theatre

📍H2 🏛1215 U St, NW
Ⓜ U Street/African Amer Civil War Memorial/Cardozo 🕐10am-6pm Mon-Fri 🔒Federal hols 🌐thelincolndc.com

Built in 1922, the Lincoln was once the centerpiece of cultural life for the city's African American community. Like the landmark 1914 Apollo Theater in New York, the Lincoln presented big-name entertainment, such as pre-eminent jazz singers Ella Fitzgerald and Billie Holiday, and composer, pianist, jazz bandleader, and native Washingtonian Duke Ellington.

By the 1960s the area around the theater began to deteriorate, and by the 1970s the theater had closed down. Then, in the early 1980s, fundraising began for the $10 million renovation. Even the original, highly elaborate plasterwork was carefully cleaned and repaired, and the theater reopened in 1994.

Today, the Lincoln Theatre is a center for the performing arts, and is one of the cornerstones of the renaissance of U Street. The magnificent

→

The Woodrow Wilson House interior with its period furnishings

auditorium plays host to a year-around calendar of concerts, stage shows, and events, including Filmfest DC.

13

Woodrow Wilson House

📍D3 🏛2340 S St, NW
Ⓜ Dupont Circle 🕐10am-4pm Wed-Sat, noon-4pm Tue and Sun (summer: to 8pm Thu) 🔒Federal hols 🌐woodrowwilsonhouse.org

The former home of Woodrow Wilson (1856–1924), who was the president of the US from 1913 to 1921, is the only presidential museum within the District of Columbia.

Wilson led the US through World War I and advocated the formation of the League of Nations, the precursor to the United Nations. In 1919 Wilson collapsed from a stroke and became incapacitated for the rest of his life. Many believe that Wilson's second wife, Edith Galt, assumed many of the presidential duties herself. Unable to leave his sickbed, Wilson saw his dream, the League of Nations, defeated in the Senate.

In 1920 Wilson was awarded the Nobel Peace Prize for his work on the League of Nations, and, at the end of his second term in 1921, he and his wife moved to this townhouse, designed by Waddy B. Wood. Edith Galt Wilson arranged for the home to be bequeathed to the nation. Since Wilson's death in 1924, the building has been maintained as it was during his lifetime, containing artifacts such as his Rolls-Royce and reflecting the style of an upper-middle-class home of the 1920s. The house today belongs to the National Trust for Historic Preservation.

A LONG WALK
EMBASSY ROW

Distance 4 km (2.5 miles) **Time** 45 minutes
Nearest Metro Dupont Circle

For fans of eclectic architecture, this walk is a fascinating experience that covers a range of styles from Georgian-Revival to Romanesque and Turkish. Starting off west from Dupont Circle, it takes you along Massachusetts Avenue, past many of the larger embassies to the Italian Embassy and then through Kalorama, a quiet residential area where smaller embassies and museums are tucked away in its tree-lined streets.

Locator Map
For more detail see p148

The **Islamic Center**, *a stunning mosque with a 160-ft (48-m) minaret*

The **Italian Embassy**, *a contemporary structure designed by architect Piero Sartogo*

WHITEHAVEN STREET NW

Italian Embassy

30TH STREET NW

ROCK CREEK DRIVE NW

MASSACHUSETTS

Islamic Center

BELMONT ROAD NW

Dumbarton Oaks Park

ROCK

Japanese Embassy

CREEK

PARKWAY

AVENUE

Rock

The **Japanese Embassy** *is a simple and graceful Georgian-Revival building.*

↑ The Italian Embassy, sitting at the top of Embassy Row

Did You Know?

The former Turkish Embassy was home to the Ertegün brothers, who co-founded Atlantic records.

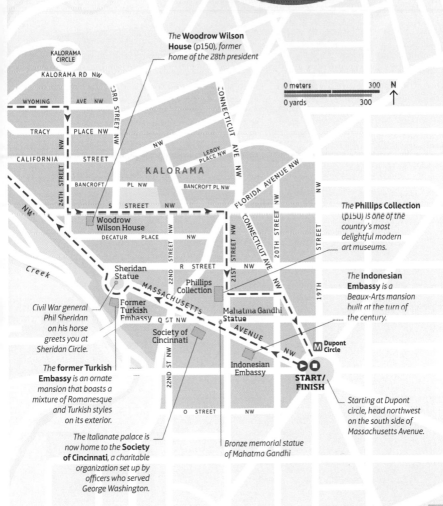

The **Woodrow Wilson House** (p150), former home of the 28th president

The Dupont Circle Fountain in Washington, DC

KALORAMA CIRCLE

KALORAMA RD NW

WYOMING AVE NW

TRACY PLACE NW

CALIFORNIA STREET

BANCROFT PL NW

BANCROFT PL NW

KALORAMA

LEROY PLACE NW

CONNECTICUT AVE NW

FLORIDA AVENUE NW

S STREET NW

Woodrow Wilson House

DECATUR PLACE NW

Sheridan Statue

R STREET NW

Phillips Collection

MASSACHUSETTS

Former Turkish Embassy

Society of Cincinnati

Q ST NW

AVENUE

Mahatma Gandhi Statue

Indonesian Embassy

O STREET NW

Creek

24TH STREET NW

3RD STREET NW

22ND STREET NW

22ND ST NW

21ST STREET NW

CONNECTICUT AVE

20TH STREET NW

19TH STREET NW

0 meters 300
0 yards 300

N ↑

The **Phillips Collection** (p150) is one of the country's most delightful modern art museums.

The **Indonesian Embassy** is a Beaux-Arts mansion built at the turn of the century.

Civil War general Phil Sheridan on his horse greets you at Sheridan Circle.

The **former Turkish Embassy** is an ornate mansion that boasts a mixture of Romanesque and Turkish styles on its exterior.

The Italianate palace is now home to the **Society of Cincinnati**, a charitable organization set up by officers who served George Washington.

Bronze memorial statue of Mahatma Gandhi

M Dupont Circle

START/ FINISH

Starting at Dupont circle, head northwest on the south side of Massachusetts Avenue.

BEYOND THE CENTER

A group of remarkable attractions lies scattered just beyond downtown. Arlington and Alexandria, settled in the early 17th century, were originally part of the British colony of Virginia, the site of vast plantations; they went on to become some of DC's first suburbs. To the south, Mount Vernon, George Washington's plantation, remains much as it was in his day. The National Cathedral to the north is arguably the city's most astounding and beautiful building, while the cheerful National Zoo nearby is perfect for kids. To the east is the National Arboretum, a 434-acre (175-ha) wonderland. In Anacostia, the Frederick Douglass National Historic Site is the home of the formerly enslaved man who became a statesman and presidential advisor.

Must Sees

1. Arlington National Cemetery
2. Mount Vernon
3. Washington National Cathedral
4. Old Town Alexandria

Experience More

5. The Pentagon
6. National Zoo
7. President Lincoln's Cottage
8. Theodore Roosevelt Island
9. Iwo Jima Memorial (US Marine Corps War Memorial)
10. Hillwood Estate Museum and Gardens
11. Rock Creek Park
12. Kenilworth Park and Aquatic Gardens
13. National Arboretum
14. Frederick Douglass National Historic Site
15. Anacostia Community Museum
16. National Harbor

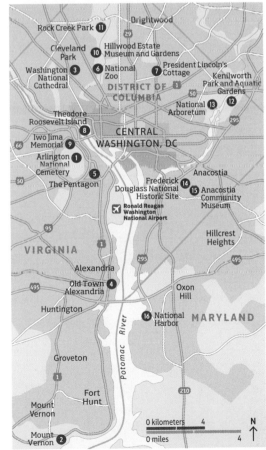

ARLINGTON NATIONAL CEMETERY

ⓘ Ⓜ 🛍

📍B9 🏛Arlington, VA Ⓜ Arlington Cemetery 🕐Oct-Mar: 8am-5pm daily; Apr-Sep: 8am-7pm daily ⓦarlingtoncemetery.mil

This is the nation's most revered military cemetery. Its imposing rolling lawns are home to rows of white headstones and the Tomb of the Unknown Soldier – symbols of sacrifices made for freedom – and the grave of President John F. Kennedy.

Today, it is sobering to stroll through the Arlington National Cemetery's 639 acres (259 ha), where a sea of white headstones marks 400,000 graves of soldiers, sailors, and airmen who gave their lives in conflicts starting from the Revolution to the present day. The so-called "Lawns of Graves" are arranged in regular grids, spread across the grounds. Although only a small percentage of Americans who have died in war lie here, the expanse gives a tangible picture of the human cost of war. Blooming magnolias and iconic cherry blossom trees add a stunning floral tribute in the springtime. Visits begin at the Welcome Center, which is located by the main cemetery entrance (on Memorial Drive). It features a bookstore as well as exhibits that tell the story of the site and its significance to the nation.

Did You Know?

In 1912, First Lady Helen Taft planted the cherry blossom trees that bloom each spring.

↑ Entrance to the Arlington House, also known as the Robert E. Lee Memorial

Memorial Amphitheater

▷ This 1920 marble amphitheater is the setting for the Memorial Day (p40), Easter sunrise service, and Veterans Day (p41) ceremonies.

Arlington House

Robert E. Lee's 1861 mansion was confiscated by the Union after he left to lead the Confederate armies in the Civil War. In 1864 the Arlington National Cemetery was created to cope with the mass death in war, and Lee never returned.

Tomb of the Unknown Soldier

▽ This 1921 memorial inside the Memorial Amphitheater honors the unidentified soldiers who have died in battle from World War I onwards.

Tuskegee Airmen Memorial Tree and Plaque

The Tuskegee Airmen, made up primarily of African American pilots, completed more than 1,800 missions during World War II. Around 355 were deployed overseas, and 84 lost their lives between 1943 and 1945.

President John F. Kennedy's Gravesite

▷ The grave of President Kennedy, who was assassinated in 1963, features an eternal flame that was lit by his wife, Jackie, during his funeral. Jackie and brothers Robert and Ted Kennedy are also buried nearby.

Activist Medgar Evers's Gravesite

Activist Medgar Evers was assassinated in 1963 by a Ku Klux Klan member in Jackson, Mississippi. He was buried here with full military honors.

Space Shuttle Memorials

A memorial honors the astronauts who died in the 1986 space shuttle *Challenger* disaster, while another memorial nearby is dedicated to the crew lost in the 2003 *Columbia* shuttle tragedy.

↑ Rows of gravestones amid cherry blossom trees at the Arlington National Cemetery

2 ⚜ 🏇 🍴 🖥 🛍

MOUNT VERNON

📍 P5 🏠 3200 Mount Vernon Memorial Hwy, VA (distillery on State Rte 235 S)
Ⓜ Huntington 🚌 Fairfax Connector 101 🕐 9am–5pm daily (Nov–Mar: to 4pm)
🌐 mountvernon.org

This graceful plantation house is the second most visited historic residence in America after the White House. No other place better portrays the character of the first US president, or the role of slavery-based agriculture in the young republic.

This country estate on the Potomac was George and Martha Washington's home for 45 years. The house was built as a farmhouse by his father, Augustine, but Washington made many changes, including adding the cupola and curving colonnades. The house is furnished as it would have been during Washington's presidency (1789–97), and visitors can explore its rooms, including the New Room, kitchen, Washington's study, and his bedroom, which contains the bed in which he died. The 500-acre (202-ha) grounds retain aspects of Washington's farm, with paddocks, stables, kitchen gardens, smokehouse, and the enslaved people's quarters. The estate's wharf, once bustling with plantation shipping, still docks tour boats from the city. The orientation center and museum make fascinating bookends to a visit, with exhibits about Washington's life and career.

> 💬 INSIDER TIP
> **Watching History**
>
> Watch reenactments at the estate, including exciting restagings of wars and battles and a recreation of George Washington's funeral. Check Mount Vernon's website for details.

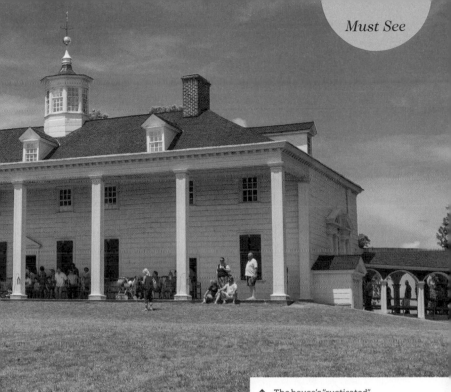

↑ The house's "rusticated" pine facade and huge river-facing portico that was the president's own design

↓ George Washington's Mount Vernon Estate

Visitors can tour the mansion, including the study and the large dining room, as well as Washington's bedroom and the bed in which he died.

Kitchen Set slightly apart from the main house, the kitchen has been completely restored.

Coach house

Boats from central DC bring visitors to this wharf. Potomac cruise boats also stop off here.

Stable

George and Martha Washington's tomb was completed in 1831

Overseer's house

The Lower Garden was used for growing berries and vegetables. The boxwood bushes around it were planted in Washington's time.

The Bowling Green was added to the estate by George Washington.

Reconstructed quarters show the living conditions of the enslaved people.

The plants and flowers in the colorful Upper Garden are known to have grown here in Washington's time.

③ ✎ Ⓜ 🖵 🛍

WASHINGTON NATIONAL CATHEDRAL

📍N3 🏛3101 Wisconsin & Massachusetts Aves, NW
Ⓜ Tenleytown/AU, Cleveland Park, then 25-min walk
🚌32, 34, 36 🕐Times vary, check website 🌐cathedral.org

The spiritual heart of the Episcopal Church in America, Washington National Cathedral is the sixth largest cathedral in the world. Built on high ground, it dominates the city skyline and is DC's highest point.

💬 INSIDER TIP
Specialty Tours

For ghouls, gargoyles, and grotesques, grab your binoculars and join the summertime tour exploring the whimsical carvings. Other tours include a tower climb, special photography access, a behind-the-scenes tour, in-depth tours on specialized topics, and a tea tour with scones and tea.

The building of the Cathedral Church of Saint Peter and Saint Paul (its official name) began in 1907 and was completed in 1990. Built with Indiana limestone, the Washington National Cathedral boasts elements typical of Gothic religious architecture, including soaring vaulting, stained-glass windows, and intricate carvings. The exterior features fanciful gargoyles and dramatic sculpture. The cathedral has been the venue for funeral and memorial services for several US presidents.

↓ The Washington National Cathedral

Pilgrim Observation Gallery

Ex Nihilo by Frederick Hart above the central portal, depicting people emerging from a swirling background

TOP 5 GARGOYLES AND OTHER GROTESQUES

Darth Vader (north)
Installed in 1986 on the cathedral's "dark" side.

Master Carver (north)
Salute to the cathedral's master carver Roger Morigi, holding a pistol, dagger, and flask in a tongue-in-cheek nod to Morigi's Italian heritage.

Yuppie (west)
A gargoyle grasping a briefcase, in honor of a New York executive.

Bishop (south)
A bishop wearing a stole and holding a crozier.

Evil Too (south)
A winged humanoid with its fingers in its ears, symbolizing evil refusing to listen to God.

The west facade, dominated by three huge Gothic arches with pierced bronze gates

George Washington Bay

1. Medieval walled gardens were the model for the cathedral's beautiful, serene Bishop's Garden.

2. Possibly the most popular sight here, Vader was the result of a design competition for children.

3. The "Creation" rose window in the west facade celebrates the majesty and mystery of creation and includes every color the artists could produce.

Pinnacles, decorated with leaf-shaped ornaments and topped by carved finials

The high altar, with 110 figures surrounding the central statue of Christ

The Children's Chapel, built to the scale of a six-year-old, with statues of Jesus as a boy, and baby and mythical animals

The Space Window, with a piece of moon rock, marking mankind's scientific achievements

The nave, with iconography telling the story of humanity

The south rose window, depicting "The Church Triumphant"

Did You Know?

There are recitals at 12:30pm most Mondays and Wednesdays on the magnificent Aeolian-Skinner organ.

↑ Colonial houses lining the tree-shaded streets of Old Town Alexandria

④

OLD TOWN ALEXANDRIA

**◉ P5 ⌂ Alexandria, 8 miles (13 km) S of Capitol Hill
🚉 Alexandria Union Station Ⓜ King St-Old Town
ℹ 221 King St, www.visitalexandriava.com**

Old Town Alexandria retains the flavor of its mid-1700s origins as a port town. Its tree-lined streets are filled with historic sights and the city remains a popular boating hub. Restaurants are abundant here, art thrives, and the socializing goes on day and night in and around the pleasant Market Square.

① ⊘ ⊗ 🕁

Carlyle House

⌂ 121 N Fairfax St ⏰ 10am-4pm Mon, Tue & Thu-Sat, noon-4pm Sun ⊘ Jan 1, Thanksgiving, Dec 24, Dec 25 🌐 novaparks.com/parks/carlyle-house-historic-park

An elegant Georgian Palladian mansion, this was built by wealthy Scottish merchant John Carlyle in 1753. It fell into disrepair in the 19th century but was bought in 1970 by the Northern Virginia Regional Park Authority and has since been beautifully restored. A tour provides fascinating details about 18th-century daily life. The garden has 18th-century plant species.

② ⊘ ⊗ 🕁

Stabler-Leadbeater Apothecary Museum

⌂ 105 S Fairfax St ⏰ Times vary, check website 🌐 alexandriava.gov/apothecary

Established in 1792, this family apothecary was in business for 141 years and is now a museum. Mahogany drawers still contain the potions noted on their labels, jars of herbal remedies line the shelves, and huge mortars and pestles and a collection of glass baby bottles are among its 8,000 original objects. George Washington was a patron, as was Robert E. Lee, who bought the paint for his Arlington house here.

③ ⊘ ⊗ 🕁 🍴 🕁

Gadsby's Tavern Museum

⌂ 134 N Royal St ⏰ Times vary, check website 🌐 alexandriava.gov/gadsbystavern

Dating from 1785, this pleasant tavern and the adjoining hotel, owned by John Gadsby, were the Waldorf-Astoria of their day. Now completely restored, they evoke the atmosphere of an old-time hostelry in this busy port. You can see the dining room with gaming tables, the bedrooms where travelers reserved not the room but a space in a bed, and the private dining room for the wealthy. The ballroom, where George and Martha Washington were fêted on his last birthday in 1799, can be rented out. This is also a working restaurant.

Did You Know?

The city is named after Scotsman John Alexander, who purchased the land on which it was built in 1669.

(4)

Torpedo Factory Art Center

- 105 N Union St
- 10am-6pm daily (to 9pm Thu)
- Jan 1, Easter, Jul 4, Thanksgiving, Dec 25
- torpedofactory.org

Built as a torpedo factory during World War II, this was converted into an arts center by a partnership between the town and a group of local artists in 1974. Today there is gallery and studio space for over 80 artists to create and exhibit their work. Visitors can watch potters, sculptors, printmakers, and jewelry-makers at their craft.

(5)

Old Presbyterian Meeting House

- 323 S Fairfax St
- 8:15am-4:15pm Mon-Fri
- opmh.org

Memorial services for George Washington were held in this 1772 meeting house. In the churchyard are buried Dr. John Craig, Washington's friend; the Reverend Muir, who officiated at Washington's funeral; and the American Revolution's unknown soldier.

(6)

Lee-Fendall House

- 614 Oronoco St
- 10am-4pm Wed-Sat, 1-4pm Sun
- leefendallhouse.org

Philip Fendall built this stylish house in 1785, then married the sister of Revolutionary War hero "Light Horse" Harry Lee. Lee's descendants lived here until 1904. Artifacts from the Revolution to the 1930s Labor Movement fill the house.

(7)

Christ Church

- 118 North Washington St
- 9am-4pm Mon-Sat, 2-4:30pm Sun
- Jan 1, Thanksgiving, Dec 25
- historicchristchurch.org

The oldest continuously used church in town, this Georgian edifice was completed in 1773. George Washington's square pew still has his nameplate, as does Robert E. Lee's.

(8)

Farmers Market

- 301 King St, Market Sq
- 7am-noon Sat

Dating back to 1753, just a few years after the city's founding in 1749, the oldest, continuous farmers' market in the US now sells fresh fruit and vegetables, herbs, meats, baked goods, cut flowers, and crafts. George Washington, a trustee of the market, regularly sent produce to be sold at the market from his farm at Mount Vernon *(p162)*.

Pier near the Torpedo Factory Art Center, Old Town Alexandria

WARNING
THIS AREA IS UNDER VIDEO SURVEILLANCE
BY THE CITY OF ALEXANDRIA
ALL ACTIVITY IS RECORDED
ILLEGAL ACTIVITY INCLUDING
TRESPASSING WILL BE PROSECUTED

EXPERIENCE MORE

5

The Pentagon

📍P4 🏛1000 Defense Pentagon, Hwy I-395, Arlington, VA Ⓜ Pentagon 🕐 For tours 10am–4pm Mon–Thu, noon–4pm Fri 🌐 pentagontours.osd.mil

The Department of Defense, which includes the army, navy, and air force, is headquartered at the Pentagon. Construction of the building was started on September 11, 1941 and completed in January, 1943. On September 11, 2001, the building was damaged in a terrorist attack. The National 9/11 Pentagon Memorial to the 184 people who died here was dedicated on September 11, 2008. Tours of the Pentagon are by appointment only and need to be booked at least 14 days in advance.

6

National Zoo

📍P3 🏛3001 Connecticut Ave, NW Ⓜ Cleveland Park, then 15 min walk, Woodley Park-Zoo/Adams Morgan 🕐 Times vary, check website 🌐 nationalzoo.si.edu

The National Zoo is home to over 1,500 animals from 300 different species, many of which are endangered. The zoo's most popular residents are giant pandas Tian Tian, Mei Xiang and Xiao Qi Ji. Set in a landscaped urban park designed by Frederick Law Olmsted in the 1890s, the zoo runs many conservation and breeding programs, the most successful of which are for the cheetahs and pandas.

→ The Hillwood Estate Museum and Gardens

7

President Lincoln's Cottage

📍P2 🏛140 Rock Creek Church Rd, NW Ⓜ Brookland-CUA 🕐 9:30am–4:30pm daily 🌐 lincolncottage.org

During the hot, stressful summers of the American Civil War, President Abraham Lincoln moved his family out of the White House and into this Gothic Revival cottage, known as the Soldiers' Home. It was here that he composed the Emancipation Proclamation in 1862, and spent his last days before he was assassinated by John Wilkes Booth in 1865. The visitor center displays various exhibits that chronicle the history of the house and Lincoln's time here.

8

Theodore Roosevelt Island

📍C6 🏛GW Memorial Pkwy, McLean, VA Ⓜ Rosslyn 🕐 6am–10pm daily 🌐 nps.gov/this

A haven for naturalists, this island's 91 acres (37 ha) of

> 🏔 GREAT VIEW
> ### From the Iwo Jima Memorial
> One of the best views in DC takes in the Lincoln Memorial, Washington Monument, US Capitol, and the National Mall. It is one of the best places to watch the fireworks on the Fourth of July.

marshland and forest are home to a variety of wildlife, trees, and plants. There are 2 miles (4 km) of nature trails, popular with bird-watchers. A bronze memorial statue honors President Theodore Roosevelt (1858–1919), who was an avid outdoorsman and promoter of national parks.

9

Iwo Jima Memorial (US Marine Corps War Memorial)

📍B7 🏛Meade St between Arlington National Cemetery & Arlington Blvd Ⓜ Rosslyn

The horrific battle of Iwo Jima that took place during World War II was captured by press

A pretty stone bridge crossing Rock Creek in Rock Creek Park ↑

photographer Joe Rosenthal. His Pulitzer Prize-winning picture of six US Marines raising the American flag on the tiny Pacific island was magnificently translated into bronze by sculptor Felix DeWeldon in 1954.

10

Hillwood Estate Museum and Gardens

📍P2 🏠4155 Linnean Ave, NW Ⓜ Van Ness-UDC 🕐10am–5pm Tue–Sun 🚫Jan, Federal hols 🌐hillwoodmuseum.org

The 25-acre (10-ha) Hillwood Estate contains the most comprehensive collection of 18th- and 19th-century Russian imperial art outside of Russia, including Fabergé eggs and Russian Orthodox Icons, plus some famous pieces of 18th-century French decorative art.

11

Rock Creek Park

📍P2 Ⓜ Cleveland Park 🌐nps.gov/rocr

Named for the creek flowing through it, the park is a 1,800-acre (728-ha) stretch of land that bisects the city from the Maryland border to the Potomac. It has a feeling of the wilderness, and foxes and deer are found in abundance. There are hiking and horse trails, a riding stable, tennis courts, a golf course, and the **Rock Creek Park Nature Center**. In the summer, the Carter Barron Amphitheater has rock, pop, jazz, and classical concerts. On Sundays, a portion of Beach Drive, one of the park's main roads, is closed to cars to give cyclists and skaters freedom of the road.

Built in 1829, **Peirce Mill** was an active gristmill, driven by the creek's tumbling waters. Today, it is a working restoration, offering demonstrations from April to October. A large, elegant stone barn next to the mill serves as an art gallery.

Rock Creek Park Nature Center

📍P2 🏠5200 Glover Rd, NW Ⓜ Friendship Heights 🚌E4 🕐9am–5pm Wed–Sun 🚫Federal hols

Peirce Mill

📍P2 🏠2401 Tilden St, NW Ⓜ Van Ness-UDC 🕐Times vary, check website 🌐nps. gov/places/peirce-mill.htm

EAT & DRINK

2Amys
Family-friendly landmark with wood-fired Neapolitan pizza and Italian wines.

📍N2 🏠3715 Macomb St, NW 🌐2amyspizza.com.

$$$⑤

Barley Mac
This chic industrial space serves American classics with a modern twist.

📍A6 🏠1600 Wilson Blvd, Arlington 🌐barleymacva.com

$$$

3321 Bistro
A popular diner specializing in Tex-Mex and Latin American food.

📍P3 🏠3321 Connecticut Ave, NW 🌐3321bistro.com

$$⑤

The Walrus Oyster and Ale
Extensive seafood menu features ten or more oyster varieties daily.

📍P5 🏠152 Waterfront St, Oxon Hill 🌐walrus oysterandale.com

$$$

Nanny O'Brien's
Traditional Irish pub with Guinness on tap and good pub food.

📍P3 🏠3319 Connecticut Ave, NW 🌐nannyobriens.com

$$⑤

⑫ Ⓜ 🛍
Kenilworth Park and Aquatic Gardens

📍 Q3 🏠 1550 Anacostia Ave, NE Ⓜ Deanwood ⏰ 9am–5pm daily (Nov–Mar: 8am–4pm) 🚫 Jan 1, Thanksgiving, Dec 25 🌐 nps.gov/keaq

This tranquil park has 12 acres (5 ha) of natural wetland areas and ponds filled with water lilies and other aquatic plants. The park was purchased in 1880 by Walter Shaw and his daughter Helen Fowler, who created the 20 or so ponds that are the centerpiece of Kenilworth. In late summer, the ponds are covered with pink blossoms. Wildlife includes otters, turtles, frogs, salamanders, and water birds. There are daily history and nature tours, and in the fall, weekend bird-watching tours.

⑬ Ⓜ 🛍
National Arboretum

📍 Q3 🏠 3501 New York Ave or 24th & R Sts off Bladensburg Rd, NE Ⓜ Stadium-Armory, then bus B2 ⏰ 8am–5pm daily 🚫 Dec 25 🌐 usna.usda.gov

Tucked away in a corner of northeast Washington, DC is the hidden gem of the National Arboretum – a center for research, education, and the preservation of trees,

↑ A pretty pagoda in the Japanese Garden at the National Arboretum

shrubs, flowers, and other plants. This is a great place for families, offering a tram tour, grassy expanses perfect for a picnic, and lovely gardens. If you are lucky enough to be here in late April, the Azalea Collections boast thousands of brilliantly colored blooms across the forest floor and along the footpaths of a wooded hillside.

The Japanese Garden includes the National Bonsai and Penjing Museum, with bonsai up to 380 years old. The herb garden has ten specialty gardens, grouping herbs according to use and historical significance. At the entrance to the garden is an elaborate 16th-century European-style "knot garden," with about 200 varieties of old

roses. The Ellipse Meadow features the National Capitol Columns, comprising 22 Corinthian columns that were once part of the US Capitol.

⑭
Frederick Douglass National Historic Site

📍 Q4 🏠 1411 W St, SE Ⓜ Anacostia ⏰ 9am–5pm Fri & Sat 🚫 Jan 1, Thanksgiving, Dec 25 🌐 nps.gov/frdo

The African American abolitionist leader Frederick Douglass lived in Washington, DC toward the end of his illustrious career. After the Civil War he moved first to a townhouse on Capitol Hill, and then to Anacostia. In 1877 he bought this white-framed house, named it Cedar Hill, and lived here, with his family, until his death in 1895. During his time here, he made many improvements and, by the time of his death, Cedar Hill had grown to a 21-room mansion.

Douglass's widow opened the house for public tours in 1903, and in 1962 the house was donated to the National Park Service. Most of the items on display are original and include gifts to Douglass from President Lincoln and the writer Harriet Beecher Stowe, author of *Uncle Tom's Cabin* (1852).

The garden has a small building that Douglass used as a study, and which he nicknamed "The Growlery." From the front steps of the house there is a magnificent view across the Anacostia River.

⑮
Anacostia Community Museum

📍 Q4 🏠 1901 Fort Place, SE Ⓜ Anacostia ⏰ 11am–4pm Tue-Sat 🌐 anacostia.si.edu

Part of the Smithsonian, this museum examines the everyday issues that impact diverse

---

FREDERICK DOUGLASS (1818-95)

Born into slavery around 1818, Frederick Douglass fought to end slavery in the United States. At the age of 20 he fled to Europe where British friends in the anti-slavery movement bought him from his masters, making him a free man. He lived mostly in New York, where he worked as a spokesman for the abolitionist movement. In 1847 he became editor of the anti-slavery newspaper *The North Star*. During the Civil War, Douglass advised President Lincoln and fought for constitutional amendments to guarantee equal rights to freed Black people.

urban communities. The art, artifacts, photographs, documents, and sound recordings displayed here reflect the lives of the people living in the largely African American and multiethnic neighborhoods east of the Anacostia River in Washington, DC. The museum hosts innovative exhibitions that are curated with the collaboration of members of the public.

With an extensive library and computers for visitors, the museum is as much a resource center as it is a space for art and history exhibitions.

INSIDER TIP
Oxon Cove Park

Stroll or cycle the paths through the forest and fields of Oxon Cove Park, set about 3 miles (5 km) north of National Harbor. The park is also a great place for a picnic.

---

16 (Ⓨ) (▭) (Ⓑ)
National Harbor

📍P5 🏠165 Waterfront St, National Harbor, MD Ⓜ King St-Old Town, Huntington, then bus Ⓦ nationalharbor.com

A glittering mini-city rising above the Potomac south of DC, National Harbor is a thriving center for shopping, dining, and entertainment. A waterfront walkway traces the edge of the river, inviting visitors to stroll past the marina and open plazas. The Capital Wheel is a favorite with older kids and a colorful carousel appeals to the little ones. In summer, there are free outdoor concerts and a giant screen that shows free movies. There are several ways to get out on the water, including kayak and canoe rentals, water taxis, and cruise boats. Nearby, the $1.3 billion MGM National Harbor luxury resort features a hotel, casino, and several restaurants.

STAY

Glover Park Hotel Georgetown

Serene luxury, attentive service, and coastal Italian cuisine in the onsite restaurant, Glover Park Grill.

📍N3 🏠2505 Wisconsin Ave, NW Ⓦ gloverparkhotel.com

$ⓈⓈⓈ

AC Hotel by Marriott National Harbor

Sophisticated riverfront hotel at National Harbor, with chic rooms and suites, fitness center, and an outdoor terrace with river views.

📍P5 🏠156 Waterfront St, Oxon Hill, MD Ⓦ marriott.com

$ⓈⓈⓈ

↑ The enormous Capital Wheel dominating the National Harbor waterfront walkway

DAYS OUT FROM WASHINGTON, DC

Within a short day's drive of Washington, DC lies enough history and natural beauty to satisfy the most insatiable sightseer. This area of Virginia and Maryland, along with parts of West Virginia and Pennsylvania, was once at the heart of the Powhatan Confederacy, comprising over 30 Algonquian-speaking Native American tribes. Founded in 1607, Jamestown was the first permanent English settlement in America, and boomed eventually due to tobacco plantations and the introduction of slavery. Relations between the British colonists and the Powhatan people quickly deteriorated, and by the mid-17th century the Powhatan Confederacy was dissolved. Today, Historic Jamestowne and nearby Colonial Williamsburg are both major attractions, with Williamsburg boasting 500 restored buildings and scores of costumed reenactors who bring the Colonial period to life. Chesapeake Bay and Annapolis are must-sees for history buffs, and both offer a wealth of dining and shopping opportunities. Lovers of the outdoors will find lots to do in Great Falls Park and on the islands of Chincoteague and Assateague. A drive west leads to the 105-mile (170-km) Skyline Drive, which offers stunning Blue Ridge Mountain scenery.

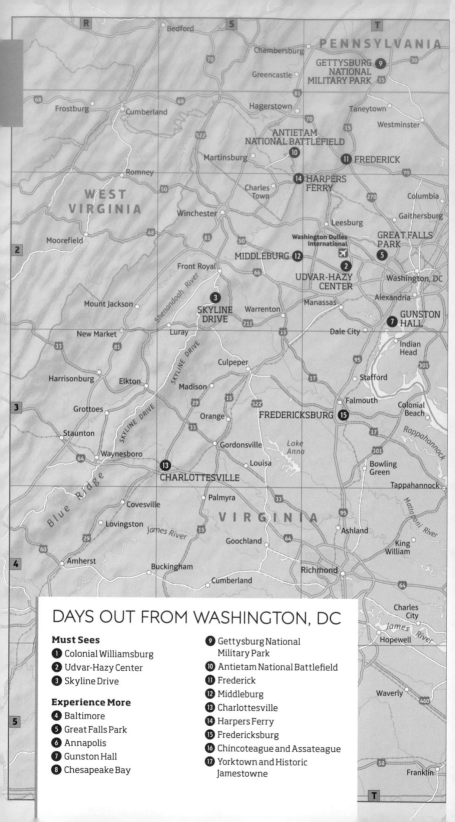

DAYS OUT FROM WASHINGTON, DC

❶ 🛡️ 🏍️ 🍴 💻 🏛️

COLONIAL
WILLIAMSBURG

📍U4 🚗155 miles (250 km) S of Washington, DC 🚌🚆 ℹ️101 Visitor
Center Dr; 9am–5pm daily; www.colonialwilliamsburg.com

Now the world's largest living history museum, this charming 18th-century
Colonial town takes visitors back to the time when the idea of the United
States was being born and the nascent country's ideals were being defined.

As Virginia's capital from 1699 to 1780, Williamsburg was the
hub of the British colony. After the government moved to
Richmond, the town went into decline. In 1926, John D.
Rockefeller embarked on a restoration project.
Today, in the midst of the modern city of
Williamsburg, the 18th-century town has
been recreated. Costumed interpreters
reenact the lives of the original towns-
people, craftsmen show off their skills,
horse-drawn carriages clatter through the
streets, and fife and drum bands play,
vividly evoking America's past.

→

The reconstructed Governor's
Palace, originally built in 1720

A quaint, restored ↑
neighborhood in
Colonial Williamsburg

Governor's Palace

The courthouse, built in 1770–71 and home of the county court for more than 150 years

← The historic area within the modern town of Williamsburg

The milliner shop, originally stocking imported clothes, jewelry, and toys

The Raleigh Tavern, once an important center for social, political, and commercial gatherings

The Capitol, which had the government in its West Wing and the General Court in its East Wing

NASSAU STREET

PALACE STREET

PALACE STREET

NORTH ENGLAND ST

QUEEN ST

NICHOLSON STREET

COLONIAL ST

DUKE OF GLOUCESTER STREET

The nursery, where costumed interpreters use replica tools and original techniques

Market Square, where reenactors read proclamations

The Printing Office, now a store selling authentic 18th-century foods

Did You Know?

Buildings with a Grand Union flag in front are open to the public; all others are private.

Did You Know?

The Mars Pathfinder found significant evidence that large amounts of water once existed on the red planet.

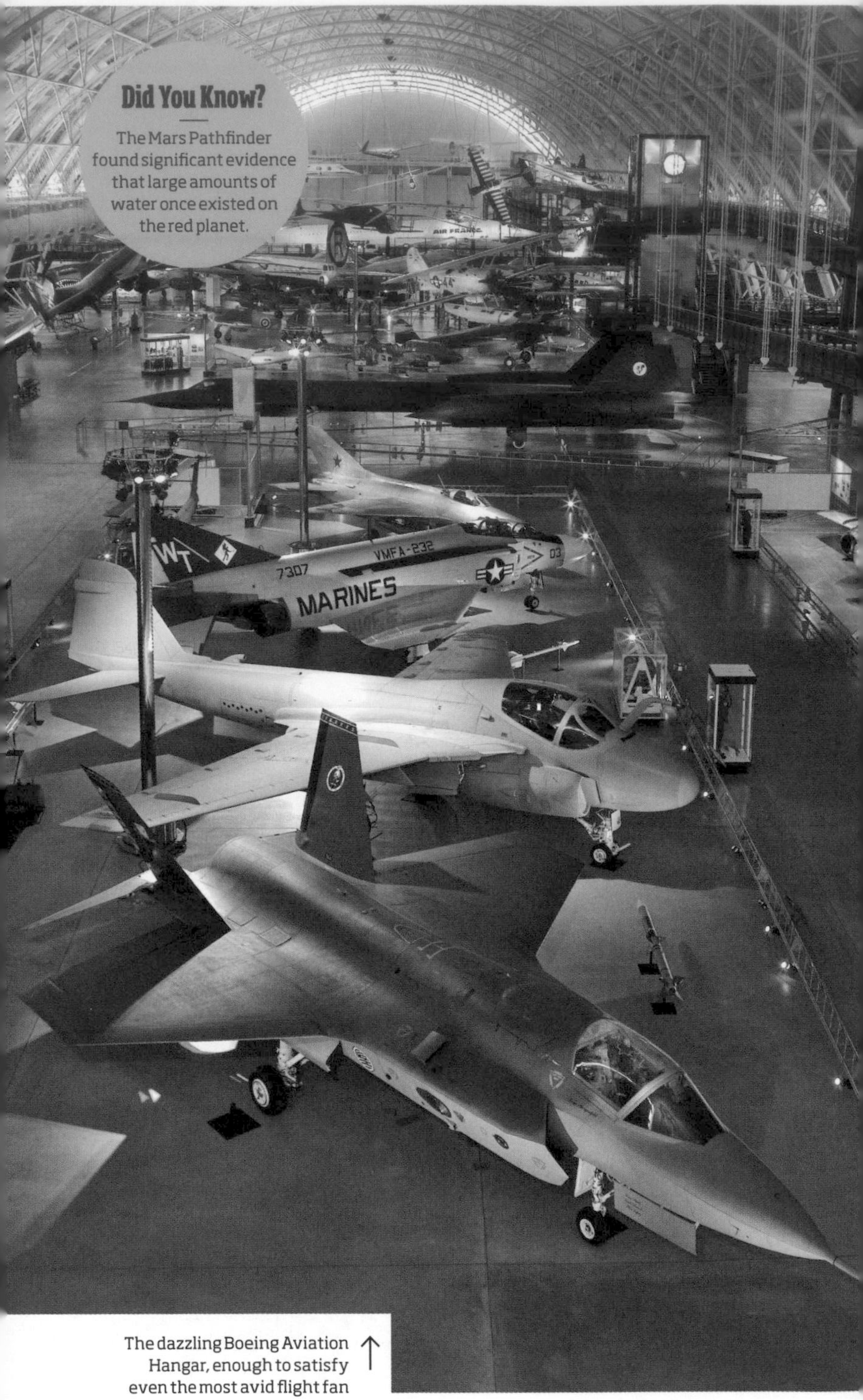

The dazzling Boeing Aviation Hangar, enough to satisfy even the most avid flight fan ↑

2 🎨 🍴 🛍️

UDVAR-HAZY CENTER

📍 T2 📍 14390 Air and Space Museum Pkwy, Chantilly, VA
Ⓜ Wiehle-Reston East, then Fairfax Connector 938
🕙 10am-5:30pm daily 🌐 airandspace.si.edu

The remarkable Steven F. Udvar-Hazy Center is a must for all enthusiasts of flight and space exploration. The museum is huge: just one of its two display hangars is the length of three football fields, ten stories high, and contains over 100 planes.

A companion to the National Air and Space Museum on the National Mall in Washington, DC *(p70)*, the center is home to the Space Shuttle *Discovery*, a Concorde supersonic jet, the B-29 Superfortress bomber *Enola Gay*, an SR-71 Blackbird spyplane, and thousands of other aviation and space artifacts. Visitors can climb up into an observation tower with a 360-degree view of nearby Dulles Airport to watch planes take off and land. Alongside the Boeing Aviation Hangar and the James S. McDonnell Space Hangar, also noteworthy is the Mary Baker Engen Restoration Hangar, where the preservation of the collection takes place. Visitors can watch restoration projects in progress from a glass-walled deck overlooking the hangar floor. Care has been taken to have plenty of kid-friendly activities, from an IMAX Theater to a squadron of flight simulators that offer experiences from a dogfight in a World War I triplane to flying a spaceship into a black hole. A Wall of Honor is a permanent testament to the men and women who have contributed to the heritage of aviation and space exploration.

TOP 5 LESSER-KNOWN AIRCRAFT AT UDVAR-HAZY

Boeing 307 Stratoliner
The first passenger airliner with a pressurized fuselage.

Pitts Special S-1C
Named *Little Stinker*, one of the most famous aerobatic planes.

Goodyear "Pilgrim" Gondola
Built in 1925 and part of Goodyear's first helium-filled airship.

Rutan Voyager
The first plane to fly nonstop around the world without a refueling stop.

Piper J-3 Cub
The most famous training craft, with thousands of pilots learning to fly in it.

1 The observation tower at the Udvar-Hazy Center is open to visitors.

2 The *Enola Gay*, a Boeing B-29 Superfortress, was the most advanced long-range bomber in World War II, and was the plane that dropped the first atomic bomb on Hiroshima, Japan.

3 The Lockheed SR-71 Blackbird, a long-range, high-altitude stealth spy plane, is the fastest jet-powered plane in the world.

The winding beauty of
Skyline Drive, one of
America's most scenic routes

3 ⊘ ⊘ ⊘ ⊘

SKYLINE DRIVE

⊙ S2 ⊕ North entrance at Front Royal, central at Thornton Gap and Swift Run Gap, south at Rockfish Gap ⊙ All year ⊘ In inclement weather ⊞ visitskylinedrive.org

One of the most beautiful and pastoral scenic drives on America's east coast, the 105-mile (170-km) Skyline Drive runs along the backbone of the Shenandoah National Park's Blue Ridge Mountains.

The road traces languidly serpentine curves high above the lush green Shenandoah River Valley, leading to 75 viewpoints that offer stunning natural scenery, as well as numerous hiking trails and points of interest. A good place to start is the Dickey Ridge visitor center from where you can get maps and guides and enjoy a splendid panoramic view of the valley. Park rangers lead a variety of hikes and programs, including a tour to the rustic camp that was President Herbert Hoover's private retreat until 1933, when he donated it to the park. Big Meadows is another popular stopping spot, with numerous hiking trails, three waterfalls, a restaurant, lodge, and campground. The large meadow for which the site was named provides a riot of color, with bright foliage in the fall and carpets of wildflowers in spring. Deer, wild turkey, black bears, bobcats, coyotes, and flying squirrels inhabit the park, and wildflowers, azaleas, and mountain laurel are abundant.

> 💬 INSIDER TIP
> **Signposting**
>
> There is no signage for sights farther afield along the drive, so a local guide can help you choose the exits that will take you to other attractions and restaurants that are located just a short distance outside Shenandoah National Park.

Did You Know?

Shenandoah National Park has over 500 miles (804 km) of hiking trails of all difficulty levels.

1 Stony Man Peak is a pleasant 1.5-mile (2.5-km) hike to rock ledges with spectacular views.

2 An iconic 0.75-mile (1.2-km) trail leads down to the lovely Dark Hollow Falls.

3 Wildlife sightings, including black bear, deer, and turkey, are common; rarer sightings include bobcat and coyote.

EXPERIENCE MORE

Baltimore

U2 **Chesapeake Bay, MD** **Inner Harbor West Wall; www.baltimore.org**

There is much to do and see in this historic city. Start at the Inner Harbor, with its waterside complex of shops and restaurants. Its focus is the **National Aquarium**, with many fascinating exhibits. The harbor is also home to the **Maryland Science Center**, where "do touch" is the rule, and the planetarium and an IMAX® theater thrill visitors. Nearby, the **American Visionary Art Museum** has works by self-taught artists whose materials range from matchsticks to faux pearls.

Known for its ancient Egyptian art, the **Walters Art Museum,** a few blocks north, also includes pieces by Monet and Fabergé. Uptown is the **Baltimore Museum of Art**, with its peerless collection of modern art, including works by Matisse, Picasso, Degas, Van Gogh, and Warhol, and two sculpture gardens featuring work by Rodin and Calder. The Little Italy area is worth a visit for its knockout Italian eateries and games of bocce (boules) played around Pratt or Stiles streets on warm nights.

National Aquarium
501 E Pratt St, Pier 3 **aqua.org**

Maryland Science Center
601 Light St **mdsci.org**

American Visionary Art Museum
800 Key Hwy at Inner Harbor **avam.org**

Walters Art Museum
600 N Charles St **thewalters.org**

Baltimore Museum of Art
10 Art Museum Drive **artbma.org**

Great Falls Park

T2 **Georgetown Pike, Great Falls, VA** **7am–dusk daily** **nps.gov/grfa**

The first view of the falls, near the visitor center, is quite breathtaking. The waters of the Potomac roar through the jagged, rocky Mather Gorge over a 76-ft (23-m) drop. Only experienced kayakers are permitted to paddle the turbulent whitewater below, which varies in power with rainfall upstream. The park boasts 15 miles (24 km) of hiking trails, some showing evidence of the commerce from the early-19th-century Patowmack, America's first canal.

> **Did You Know?**
>
> The Potomac narrows from 1,000 ft (305 m) above Great Falls to 60 ft (18 m) below, greatly increasing its force.

Annapolis

U2 **Anne Arundel County, MD** **26 West St; www.visitannapolis.org**

Maryland's capital Annapolis is the jewel of Chesapeake Bay, defined by the distinct nautical

→ Maryland State House rising above the picturesque Main Street in Annapolis

184

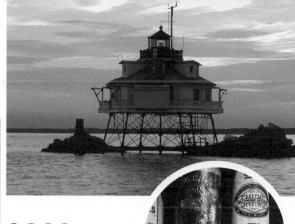

Chesapeake Bay's Thomas Point Shoal Light, and exhibits at the Chesapeake Bay Maritime Museum *(inset)*

nautical character that comes with 17 miles (27 km) of shoreline and the long-time presence of the US Naval Academy.

Main Street goes past the 200-year-old Maryland Inn to the City Dock. From here it is a short walk to the 150-year-old **US Naval Academy**, whose visitor center contains the Freedom 7 capsule that carried the first American, Alan Shepard, into space.

Annapolis teems with Colonial buildings, most of them still in everyday use. The **Maryland State House** is the oldest state capitol in continuous use. Delegates from the American colonies met here when Annapolis was briefly the nation's capital in 1783–4. **William Paca House**, home of Governor Paca, one of those who signed the Declaration of Independence, is a fine Georgian house with a pretty garden, both of which have been lovingly restored. The **Hammond Harwood House**, a Georgian masterpiece, has also been restored. The Duke of Gloucester and Cornhill streets are fine examples of the city's historic residential streets. Many tours are on offer in Annapolis, including by foot, bus, and boat.

US Naval Academy
⊘ 🏠 52 King George St
🌐 usna.edu

Maryland State House
⊘ 🏠 State Circle 🌐 msa.maryland.gov

William Paca House
⊘ 🏠 186 Prince George St
🌐 annapolis.org

Hammond Harwood House
⊘ 🏠 19 Maryland Ave at King George St 🌐 hammondharwoodhouse.org

7 🎨 🎭 🛍
Gunston Hall

📍 T2 🏠 10709 Gunston Road, Mason Neck, VA
🕐 9:30am–6pm daily
🚫 First 2 weeks of Jan, Thanksgiving, Dec 25
🌐 gunstonhall.org

This Georgian house, built in 1755, was the home of George Mason, author of the 1776 Virginia Declaration of Rights. Situated 20 miles (32 km) south of Washington, DC, it is an exquisite example of careful historic restoration. Of particular interest is the finely carved woodwork in the entrance hall, and the Chinoiserie mantel and woodwork in the formal dining room.

Outside, the gardens are lined with boxwood hedges that are more than 250 years old. Between spring and fall, visitors can also learn about the history of enslaved people at Gunston Hall with the archaeology team.

8 🍴 🍽 🛍
Chesapeake Bay

📍 U3 🌐 baydreaming.com

Called "the land of pleasant living," Chesapeake Bay offers visitors historic towns, fishing villages, bed-and-breakfasts, seafood restaurants, beaches, wildlife, and farmland. The **Chesapeake Bay Maritime Museum**, located in the small town of St. Michaels, depicts life on the bay, both past and present. **Tilghman Island**, in the middle of Chesapeake Bay, has the last commercial fleet of sailboats in North America and hosts a popular seafood festival every June.

Chesapeake Bay Maritime Museum
🌐 cbmm.org

Tilghman Island
🌐 tilghmanisland.com

DRINK

Boatyard Bar and Grill
Yacht-themed bar with award-winning seafood and the best crab cakes and sandwiches.

📍 U2 🏠 400 4th St, Annapolis, MD
🌐 boatyardbarandgrill.com
Ⓢ Ⓢ Ⓢ

THE GETTYSBURG ADDRESS

The main speaker at the dedication of the National Cemetery in Gettysburg on November 19, 1863 was the orator Edward Everett. President Lincoln had been asked to follow with "a few appropriate remarks." His two-minute, 272-word speech paid tribute to the fallen soldiers, restated his goals for the Civil War, and rephrased the meaning of democracy: "government of the people, by the people, for the people." Inaudible to many, Lincoln declared the speech a failure. However, once published, it revitalized the North's resolve to preserve the Union, and today it is known to every schoolchild in America.

9

Gettysburg National Military Park

Q T1 **A** Gettysburg, PA
C 30 mins before sunrise–30 mins before sunset
C Jan 1, Thanksgiving, Dec 25 **W** nps.gov/gett

This 10-sq-mile (25-sq-km) park, south of the town of Gettysburg, Pennsylvania, marks the site of the three-day Civil War battle on July 1–3, 1863. It remains the bloodiest event ever to take place on American soil, with 51,000 casualties. Union victory ended Confederacy hopes for independence. A two- or three-hour driving tour begins at the **visitor center**. Free ranger-led walks interpret and explain the battle. On weekends (April–October) there are Living History reenactments. Other sights include the National Cemetery opposite, where Lincoln gave his Gettysburg Address, the David Wills House where he finalized the speech, and the Eternal Light Peace Memorial.

Visitor Center
A 1195 Baltimore Pike
C Times vary, check website

10

Antietam National Battlefield

Q S1 **A** Rte 65, 10 miles (16 km) S of Hagerstown, Washington County, MD
C Dawn–dusk daily (visitor center: 9am–4pm daily)
C Jan 1, Thanksgiving, Dec 25 **W** nps.gov/anti

One of the worst battles of the Civil War was waged here on September 17, 1862. There were 23,000 dead, wounded, or missing, but no decisive victory. An observation tower offers sweeping battlefield views. Antietam Creek flows peacefully under Burnside Bridge. General Lee's defeat

→

Cannon in front of the New York State Monument, Antietam National Battlefield

inspired Lincoln to issue the Emancipation Proclamation. The visitor center has an excellent movie recreating the historic battle.

11

Frederick

Q T1 **A** Frederick County, MD **i** 151 S East St; www.visitfrederick.org

This charming town's historic downtown was beautifully restored, and is now home to hundreds of antiques dealers. The **National Museum of Civil War Medicine** displays tools and equipment used in the war to illustrate the medical practices of the time. **Rose Hill Manor Park** offers children hands-on experiences of the daily life of the first governor of Maryland and his family. Francis Scott Key, author of "The Star-Spangled Banner," is buried here in Frederick's Mount Olivet Cemetery.

National Museum of Civil War Medicine
W civilwarmed.org

Rose Hill Manor Park
W recreator.com/264

↑ Shopping street in
picturesque Middleburg

12 Ⓦ ☐ ⓐ

Middleburg

Ⓐ S2 Ⓐ Rte 50, Loudoun
County, VA Ⓘ 12 N Madison
St; open 11am–3pm daily;
www.visitmiddleburg
va.com

The horse is king in this
little piece of England nestled
in the foothills of Virginia's
Blue Ridge Mountains. The
town's history began in 1728,
with Joseph Chinn's fieldstone
tavern on the Ashby's Gap
Road, still operating as the
Red Fox Inn. The exquisite
countryside has a number

of thoroughbred horse
farms; Foxcroft Road, north
of town, winds past some. In
town, the **National Sporting
Library & Museum** special-
izes in fine art depicting
equestrian as well as other
outdoor sports.

Dozens of wineries thrive
in the area. Along John Mosby
Highway are the **Chrysalis
Vineyards** and the **Cana
Vineyards and Winery**. Both
have tours and tastings. **Aldie
Mill Historic Park** nearby has
tours of the 200-year-old mill
on summer weekends.

**National Sporting
Library & Museum**
Ⓐ 102 The Plains Road
Ⓦ nationalsporting.org

Chrysalis Vineyards
Ⓐ 39025 John Mosby Hwy
Ⓦ chrysaliswine.com

**Cana Vineyards
and Winery**
Ⓐ 38600 John Mosby Hwy
Ⓦ canavineyards.com

Aldie Mill Historic Park
Ⓐ 39401 John Mosby Hwy
Ⓦ novaparks.com

EAT

Bertha's
"Eat Bertha's Mussels"
with a pint of bitter at
this fun seafood joint.
Live music many
evenings.
Ⓐ U2 Ⓐ 734 S Broadway,
Baltimore, MD
Ⓦ berthas.com

$$$

Firestone's Culinary Tavern
Trendy gastropub with
an extensive American
menu and over 80
beers. The seared
scallops are excellent.
Ⓐ T1 Ⓐ 105 N Market St,
Frederick, MD
Ⓦ firestones
restaurant.com

$$$

Whiskey Jar
Traditional Southern
comfort food with local,
seasonal ingredients,
plus a whiskey bar.
Ⓐ S3 Ⓐ 227 W Main St,
Charlottesville, VA
Ⓦ thewhiskeyjar
cville.com

$$$

Red Hot and Blue
Memphis-style hickory
ribs and pulled pork are
served in this family-
friendly place with
blues memorabilia.
Ⓐ U2 Ⓐ 200 Old Mill
Bottom Rd S, Annapolis,
MD Ⓦ redhotandblue.
com/annapolis

$$$

Sin Fronteras
Authentic Mexican and
Latin American cuisine
served in a tiny, cheer-
ful restaurant. Great
margaritas.
Ⓐ U2 Ⓐ 2129 Forest Dr,
Annapolis, MD
Ⓦ sinfronterascafe.com

$$$

Crab Claw
This popular waterfront
restaurant serves fresh
seasonal Chesapeake
Bay seafood. Full-
service bar.
Ⓐ U2 Ⓐ 304 Burns St,
St. Michaels, MD
Ⓦ thecrabclaw.com

$$$

13 🍴 🍷 🖼 🏛

Charlottesville

📍 S3 🏛 Virginia 🚗🚆
ℹ 610 E Main St; www.
visitcharlottesville.org

Charlottesville was US president Thomas Jefferson's hometown. It is dominated by the University of Virginia, which he founded as well as designed, and by his home, **Monticello**. It is believed that more than 400 enslaved people worked at Monticello during Jefferson's lifetime, including Sally Hemings, who bore six of Jefferson's children; find out more by a tour and an exhibit exploring Hemings' life.

Since 2010, Charlottesville has been the site of local struggles between those in favor of removing Confederate symbols and those who want to keep them. Statues of American Civil War generals Robert E. Lee and Stonewall Jackson were removed from public parks in 2021.

Vineyards and wineries surround Charlottesville. **Michie Tavern** has been restored to

its 18th-century appearance, and serves a buffet of typical Southern food. **James Madison's Montpelier**, on a 2,500-acre (1,000-ha) site 25 miles (40 km) to the north, was the home of US president James Madison.

Monticello
♿ 🚻 🛍 📍 931 Thomas Jefferson Pkwy, Rte 53
🕐 Times vary, check website
🌐 monticello.org

Michie Tavern
🍴 📍 683 Thomas Jefferson Pkwy 🌐 michietavern.com

James Madison's Montpelier
♿ 🚻 🛍 📍 11350 Constitution Hwy, Montpelier Station
🌐 montpelier.org

---

14 🚗 🚲 🍷 🍴 🖼 🏛

Harpers Ferry

📍 S2 🏛 Jefferson County, WV 🕐 Times vary, check website 🌐 nps.gov/hafe

Nestled at the confluence of the Shenandoah and

Potomac rivers in the Blue Ridge Mountains is Harpers Ferry. The town, part of which is now a National Historical Park, was named for Robert Harper, a Philadelphia builder who established a ferry across the Potomac here in 1761. There are stunning views from Maryland Heights to the foot of Shenandoah Street, near abolitionist John Brown's fort. Brown's ill-fated 1859 raid on the Federal arsenal became tinder in igniting the Civil War. The historic importance of the town led to it being designated a national park in 1944.

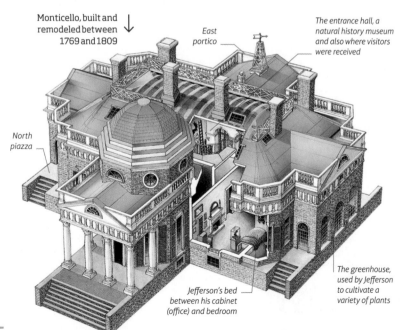

Monticello, built and remodeled between 1769 and 1809

East portico

The entrance hall, a natural history museum and also where visitors were received

North piazza

Jefferson's bed between his cabinet (office) and bedroom

The greenhouse, used by Jefferson to cultivate a variety of plants

A replica of one of the colonists' ships, Historic Jamestowne

15 🍴 💻 🛍️
Fredericksburg

📍 T3 · 🏛️ Virginia ◻️◻️
ℹ️ 706 Caroline St; times vary, check website; www.visitfred.com

The town's attractions are its historic downtown district and four Civil War battlefields. Downtown, the Hugh Mercer Apothecary Shop and Rising Sun Tavern offer living history accounts of life in a town that began as a Rappahannock River port. **Kenmore**, home of George Washington's sister Betty Washington Lewis, has some beautiful interiors.

Kenmore
♿ 🏛️ 1201 Washington Ave
🌐 kenmore.org

16
Chincoteague and Assateague

📍 V3 · 🏛️ Accomack County, VA 🌐 nps.gov/asis

These adjacent islands offer a wealth of natural beauty, and can be accessed by road from Virginia. Chincoteague is more developed, and has a town of the same name with the small **Museum of Chincoteague Island** displaying oyster-industry artifacts and oyster boats. A road from here offers access to Assateague Island, an unspoiled strip with a beach and hiking trails.

Assateague is famously populated by wild ponies. Its woodlands and salt marshes attract over 300 species of birds. There are several campgrounds in the area, and the beach is ideal for swimming and surf fishing. The **Chincoteague National Wildlife Refuge** can provide more information on accommodation and activities.

Museum of Chincoteague Island
♿ 🏛️ 7125 Maddox Blvd
🌐 chincoteaguemuseum.com

Chincoteague National Wildlife Refuge
♿ 🏛️ 8231 Beach Rd 🌐 fws.gov/refuge/chincoteague

---

17 🍴 💻 🛍️
Yorktown and Jamestown

📍 U5 · 🏛️ York County & James City County, VA
ℹ️ (757) 890-3300

Founded in 1607, Jamestown was America's first permanent English settlement. The site includes **Historic Jamestowne**, which features a museum and the ruins of the original settlement. There is a recreation of James Fort, as well as full-scale reproductions of the first colonists' ships and a Native American village.

Yorktown was the site of the decisive 1781 battle of the American Revolution. **Colonial National Historical Park**'s battlefield tours and exhibits explain the siege at Yorktown.

Historic Jamestowne
♿ 🏛️ 1368 Colonial Pkwy, Jamestown 🌐 historicjamestowne.org

Colonial National Historical Park
♿ 🏛️ 1000 Colonial Pkwy, Yorktown
🌐 nps.gov/colo

STAY

10 Clarke
Upscale Victorian B&B with a garden located in a historic area near downtown Frederick.

📍 T1 · 🏛️ 10 Clarke Pl, Frederick, MD
🌐 10clarke.com

$⑤$⑤$⑤

Inn at Court Square
Luxury boutique inn set in two adjacent houses, beautifully furnished with antiques. Free parking and breakfast.

📍 S3 · 🏛️ 410 E Jefferson St, Charlottesville, VA
🌐 innatcourtsquare.com

$⑤$⑤$⑤

NEED TO KNOW

Washington, DC Metro station

BEFORE
YOU GO

Things change, so plan ahead to make the most of your trip. Be prepared for all eventualities by considering the following points before you travel.

AT A GLANCE

CURRENCY
US Dollar (USD)

AVERAGE DAILY SPEND

SAVE	SPEND	SPLURGE
$120	**$250**	**$350+**

BOTTLED WATER	COFFEE	BEER	DINNER FOR TWO
$1.75	**$4**	**$6**	**$90**

CLIMATE

There are about 15 days of sun per month in winter, but nearly 20 days in summer.

Temperatures range from an average of 1°C (34°F) in January to 26°C (79°F) in July.

There is an average of 4 in (101 mm) of rain May through September, and it reaches its lowest ebb in late winter.

ELECTRICITY SUPPLY

The standard US electric current is 110 volts and 60 Hz. Power sockets are type A and B, fitting plugs with two flat pins.

Passports and Visas

For entry requirements, including visas, consult your nearest US embassy or check the **US Department of State** website. Canadian visitors require a valid passport to enter the US. Citizens of Australia, New Zealand, the UK, and the EU do not need a visa, but must apply in advance for the Electronic System for Travel Authorization (**ESTA**) and have a valid passport. All other visitors will need a passport and tourist visa to enter the US.
ESTA
W esta.cbp.dhs.gov
US Department of State
W travel.state.gov

Government Advice

Now more than ever, it is important to consult both your and the US government's advice before traveling. The **UK Foreign and Commonwealth Office**, the **Australian Department of Foreign Affairs and Trade**, and the **US Department of State** *(see above)* offer the latest information on security, health, and local regulations.
Australian Department of Foreign Affairs and Trade
W smartraveller.gov.au
UK Foreign and Commonwealth Office
W gov.uk/foreign-travel-advice

Customs Information

You can find information on the laws relating to goods and currency taken in or out of the US on the **US Customs and Border Protection Agency** website.
US Customs and Border Protection Agency
W cbp.gov/travel

Insurance

We recommend that you take out a comprehensive insurance policy, covering the loss of belongings, medical care, cancellations, and delays, and read the small print carefully. There is no universal healthcare in the US for citizens or visitors, and healthcare is very expensive, so it is particularly important to take out comprehensive medical insurance.

Vaccinations

No specific inoculations are required to visit the US. For information regarding COVID-19 vaccination requirements, consult government advice.

Booking Accommodations

Prices are lowest from January to March. Spring and summer are popular and generally expensive, although weekend rates may be lower when Congress is not in session. Book well in advance to secure the best deals. Rates are subject to an additional 14.95 percent room tax.

A comprehensive list of accommodations to suit all needs can be found on Destination DC, the city's official tourism website (p198).

Money

Most establishments accept major credit, debit, and prepaid currency cards. Contactless payments are becoming increasingly common, but cash is usually required by smaller shops and businesses, and by street vendors. DC's Metro services rolled out contactless payment options in 2020.

Tipping is customary. In restaurants it is normal to tip 20 percent of the total bill and $1 per drink in a bar. Allow for a tip of 15 percent for taxi drivers. Hotel porters and housekeeping expect $3–$5 per bag or day.

Travelers with Specific Requirements

Washington, DC is one of the most accessible cities in the US, but there are challenges involved with some historic buildings, restaurants, and shops.

Metrorail stations and trains are accessible, featuring extra-wide gates and elevators. Rail cars have gap reducers, priority seating, and emergency intercoms that also include instructions in Braille and raised alphabet. All Metrobuses are wheelchair friendly and have lifts or ramps for easy access. Visitors can find

more information about public transportation accessibility on the **Metro** website.

Government buildings, museums, and theaters are generally accessible, but it is always best to call ahead to ensure that any specific requirements will be met.

Destination DC (p198) provides detailed information, tips, and general assistance for visitors with specific needs.

Metro
w wmata.com/accessibility

Language

Although the main language spoken in Washington, DC is English, followed closely by Spanish, this is a cosmopolitan city in which you will hear multiple languages. Many attractions and tour companies cater to those with limited English by offering foreign-language headsets, museum guides, and information packs.

Opening Hours

COVID-19 Increased rates of infection may result in temporary opening hours and/or closures. Always check ahead before visiting museums, attractions, and hospitality venues.

Monday Many museums close on Mondays.
Sunday Most banks close at 3pm and smaller businesses close for the day.
Federal and State Holidays Many museums, public attractions, and businesses close.

FEDERAL HOLIDAYS	
Jan 1	New Year's Day
3rd Mon Jan	Martin Luther King, Jr. Day
3rd Mon Feb	President's Day
Last Mon May	Memorial Day
Jul 4	Independence Day
1st Mon Sep	Labor Day
4th Mon Nov	Thanksgiving Day
Dec 25	Christmas Day

GETTING
AROUND

Whether exploring Washington, DC's historic sights on foot or by public transportation, here is all you'll need to know to navigate the city like a pro.

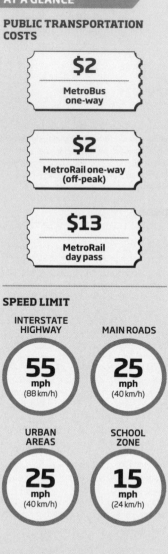

AT A GLANCE

PUBLIC TRANSPORTATION COSTS

$2
MetroBus one-way

$2
MetroRail one-way (off-peak)

$13
MetroRail day pass

SPEED LIMIT

INTERSTATE HIGHWAY
55 mph (88 km/h)

MAIN ROADS
25 mph (40 km/h)

URBAN AREAS
25 mph (40 km/h)

SCHOOL ZONE
15 mph (24 km/h)

Arriving by Air

Three major airports serve Washington, DC. International flights arrive at Dulles International Airport (IAD), internal flights arrive at Reagan National Airport (DCA), and Baltimore/Washington International Thurgood Marshall Airport (BWI) is a hub for low-cost international and internal flights.

Wiehle-Reston East is the nearest Metrorail station to Dulles, from which there is the connecting Washington Flyer Silver Line Express Bus to the airport. Travel time from the city center is over an hour. A quicker option is to take a Washington Flyer Taxicab, which serves the airport 24 hours a day.

Reagan National Airport is served by the blue and yellow Metrorail lines. Travel time to and from downtown Washington is typically around 20 minutes.

Trains run every hour from 4am to 10pm from Union Station to Baltimore/Washington International Thurgood Marshall Airport, but a cheaper option is the MARC service from Union Station, which runs every hour from 6am to 10:30pm (weekdays only).

For more information on journey times and pricing between the airport and downtown, see the table opposite.

Domestic Train Travel

Traveling by train is one of the best ways to reach the DC area. **Amtrak** is the national train operator of the US, and runs direct trains between Washington, DC and major cities, such as Baltimore, Philadelphia, Richmond, and Williamsburg. All trains arrive at the large Union Station, located near the Capitol. The station is easily accessible by Metrorail and Metrobus.

Amtrak offers a deluxe train service to New York City, called the Acela, which is faster and more comfortable than the regular train, but is more expensive. Both Acela and the slower Northeast Regional trains to New York leave every hour. **MARC**, Maryland's regional commuter train, has regular fast services to Baltimore.

GETTING TO AND FROM THE AIRPORT

Airport	Transport	Price	Journey Time
Dulles International	Washington Flyer Silver Line Express plus Metrorail	$5.00	1 hr 30 mins
	Taxi	$65-80	30 mins
Reagan National	Metrorail	from $6	20 mins
	Taxi	$10-30	20 mins
Baltimore/Washington International Thurgood Marshall	Maryland Rail Commuter Service (MARC)	from $8	35 mins
	Amtrak train	from $12	20 mins
	Taxi	$85	1 hr

If traveling widely across the country, it may be worth buying a USA Rail Pass, which gives reduced fares, and can be purchased on the Amtrak website.

Amtrak
Ⓦ amtrak.com
MARC
Ⓦ mta.maryland.gov

Public Transportation

Washington Metropolitan Area Transit Authority (**WMATA**) is Washington, DC's main public transportation provider. Safety and hygiene measures, timetables, ticket information, transport maps, and more can be obtained from the WMATA website.
WMATA
Ⓦ wmata.com

Tickets

Metrorail has phased out paper tickets in favor of SmarTrip cards and device contactless payments. Rechargeable SmarTrip cards can be used not only on Metrorail services but also on city buses and other regional transit systems. On buses you can also pay with cash: place your exact fare in coins or dollar bills in the fare box near the driver (the driver does not carry cash to make change).

SmarTrip cards can be bought and topped up online, from Metrorail vending machines at stations, or from Metro retail outlets. A SmarTrip card costs $2 and can be loaded with cash on a pay as you go basis or with various passes, including for one day ($13), three days ($28), and seven days ($58). The cost of individual fares depends on the time and distance you wish to travel. The base fare starts from $2 off-peak and $2.25 at peak times. It is more expensive to travel during rush hour. You can also pay for travel through Apple Pay or Google Pay on your smartphone.

Metrorail

For most destinations in the city, Metrorail, the subway-surface rail system, is the best way to get around. Metrorail consists of six color-coded lines: Red, Blue, Orange, Yellow, Green, and Silver. Trains run from 5am to 11:30pm Monday through Thursday, from 5am to 1am on Friday, from 7am to 1am on Saturday, and from 8am to 11pm on Sunday. Trains run frequently (every 10 minutes or less) and stops are announced at every station. Peak times (5–9:30am and 3–7pm Monday–Friday) are best avoided.

Each Metro station works on three levels: street level, where you enter; mezzanine, where ticket machines are located; and the platform, which is accessed by escalator or elevator. Use the Metro map to figure out which line you need for your destination and the terminus you will be heading for. The terminus denotes the direction the train is traveling and will be on signs in the station, guiding you to the correct platform. Where there is more than one line, follow the signs first for the line that you want and then the platform.

Tap your SmarTrip card or scan your mobile device on the reader at the rail station fare gate when entering and leaving.

Check the WMATA website for regular updates on travel disruptions and closures due to track maintenance.

MetroBus

MetroBus is a fast, inexpensive way to get around Washington, DC and connect to numerous outlying districts.

Fares can be paid either with exact change when you board the bus or with a SmarTrip card, which can be purchased online. Transfers are free within a three-hour period for SmarTrip card users. All other tickets are non-transferable; if changing buses after paying with exact change you will need to pay for a new fare. Up to two children under the age of five can travel for free with a fare-paying passenger, and there are discounts available for travelers with disabilities and senior citizens.

Bus stops are identified by red, white, and blue signs. Signs list details of routes taken by all buses that use that stop. The bus will display both the route number and its terminus. Buses do not stop automatically; you will need to flag one down at a designated stop if you wish to board. Stops are announced on board. Pull on the line running along the top of the windows to request a stop. Always exit the bus at the back.

The **DC Circulator** bus is a popular choice for visitors. It links most of Washington, DC's main sights and attractions, and runs every 10 minutes. Fares are $1 for adults and 50 cents for children (under-5s travel free with a paying adult).

Maps of all the bus routes are available in Metrorail stations, and maps of specific lines are posted at each bus stop.

DC Circulator
W dccirculator.com

Long-Distance Bus Travel

Intercity buses are an excellent, economical way to get to Washington, DC. As well as the traditional Greyhound buses, there are half a dozen bus companies serving DC, including **Megabus**, **FlixBus**, and the **Washington Deluxe**. Many of these buses are equipped with restrooms and free Wi-Fi.

Tickets are sold on a scale – a one-way ticket to New York generally costs about $30, but may end up costing as little as $1 with advance purchase, which is always cheaper than buying on the day.

Greyhound buses depart from the bus terminal near Union Station, but many of the other bus companies leave from more central locations throughout the city.

FlixBus
W flixbus.com
Greyhound
W greyhound.com
Megabus
W megabus.com
Washington Deluxe
W washny.com

Bus Tours

Several companies offer bus tours of DC's historic surroundings. **Gray Line** takes you on the Black Heritage tour, to Gettysburg National Military Park, Colonial Williamsburg, or Jefferson's home, Monticello. Several companies offer open-top tours. Passengers can hop on and off at any stop, and one- or two-day passes are available. **City Sights DC** organizes combination day trips covering Washington, DC's most popular landmarks, monuments, and points of interest.

City Sights DC
W citysightsdc.com
Gray Line
W graylinedc.com

Taxis

There are designated taxi ranks across the city. The **Department of For-Hire Vehicles** has an interactive map of taxi stands in the district. In addition, taxis wait near major sights, offices, and hotels. It is less easy to hail a taxi on the street. **DC Yellow Cab** is a reliable taxi company that can be pre-booked.

Taxi fares in DC are operated using time and distance meters. Passengers should expect to pay a starting "drop" rate of $3.50, and then $2.16 for every mile after this. Luggage, extra pick-ups, and rush hour travel can all incur surcharges. Taxis charge $25.00 per hour for waiting. Be aware that drivers do not always know the way to addresses beyond the tourist center. Taxi app companies such as Uber, Lyft, and Via also operate in the city.

DC Yellow Cab
W dcyellowcab.com
Department of For-Hire Vehicles
W dfhv.dc.gov

Driving

There is much to see beyond Washington's city limits, and traveling by car is easy with a GPS. However, driving is not the most efficient way to get around in the core DC area. Traffic congestion, one-way streets, and time-of-day parking restrictions can make driving difficult . Avoid rush hour (5–9:30am and 3–7pm Monday–Saturday), when there is not only a high volume of traffic but rush-hour tolls are imposed on some roads.

Washington, DC's road network forms a grid. Most numbered streets run north and south, and most lettered streets east and west. Diagonal streets running at a 45-degree angle crisscross the grid in both directions and have a full road name, which is usually the name of a state.

Addresses contain NE, SE, SW, or NW, indicating their position relative to the Capitol building, which is at the center of the grid. Every address in DC includes the quadrant code, and its use is necessary to distinguish the precise location you are trying to reach.

Be aware that there is no "J," "X," "Y," or "Z" Street, and "I" Street is written as "Eye" Street.

Car Rental

Rental car companies are located at airports, Union Station, and many other locations

To rent a car in the US you must be at least 25 years old with a valid driver's license and a clean record. All agencies require a major credit card.

Getting damage and liability insurance is recommended. It is advisable to return the car with a full tank of gas, otherwise you will be required to pay the inflated fuel prices charged by the rental agencies. Check for any pre-existing damage to the car and make sure you note this on your contract.

Parking

Parking in a lot will cost you about $30 per day or about $12 for two hours. Street parking meters have a two-hour maximum stay, and fines are high.

Parking is prohibited on many downtown streets during rush hour. You can find specific time restrictions signposted on curbside signs. Your car will be towed if you disregard them.

Gasoline (Petrol)

There are over a hundred gas stations in the city. Gas comes in three grades – regular, mid-range, and premium. Most stations are exclusively self-service and only accept credit cards

Rules of the Road

All drivers are required to carry a valid driver's license and must be able to produce registration documents and insurance for their vehicle. Most foreign licenses are valid, but if your license is not in English, or does not have a photo ID, you must get an International Driving Permit (IDP) in advance of your trip.

Traffic drives on the right-hand side of the road. Seat belts are compulsory in front seats and suggested in the back; children under three must ride in a child seat in the back. Belts are also compulsory in cabs.

You can turn right at a red light as long as you first come to a complete stop, and if there are no signs that prohibit it. A flashing yellow light at an intersection means slow down, look for oncoming traffic, and proceed with caution. Passing (overtaking) is allowed on any multilane road, and you must pass on the left. On smaller roads safe passing places are shown by a broken yellow line on your side of the double-yellow line.

Crossing a double-yellow line, either by U-turn or by passing the car in front, is illegal, and will incur a fine if caught.

If a school bus stops to let passengers off, all traffic from both sides must stop and wait for the bus to drive off.

A limit of 0.08 percent blood alcohol is strictly enforced. For drivers under the age of 21 there is a zero-tolerance policy for drunk-driving. Driving while intoxicated (DWI) is a punishable offense that incurs heavy fines or even a prison sentence. Do not drink if you plan to drive.

In the event of an accident or breakdown, drivers of rental cars should contact their car rental company first. Members of the American Automobile Association (**AAA**) can have their vehicle towed to the nearest service station for repairs.

AAA
🅦 aaa.com

Cycling

There is a handy network of cycle routes throughout the city, with some main roads offering dedicated cycle lanes.

Capital Bikeshare has bicycles for rent at around 500 locations. One-day, three-day, or monthly passes are available. **Bike and Roll** offers bike rentals, as well as organized tours of the city. Rentals can be made by phone or in-store from a minimum of two hours ($16) to a maximum of one day ($40). They provide helmets, some equipment such as locks, bicycle pumps, and puncture repair kits, as well as bicycle route maps of the city.

Some cycle lanes are also used by buses and taxis. Bicycles can be taken on buses, but must be stowed on racks at the front.

Bike and Roll
🅦 bikeandrolldc.com
Capital Bikeshare
🅦 capitalbikeshare.com

Walking

Washington is a city built for walking, with numerous green spaces, wide sidewalks, and courteous drivers. Busy streets have pedestrian walk lights at intersections.

While many of the main sights and monuments are clustered around the Mall, other attractions are quite spread out, so be sure to pack a pair of comfortable shoes.

Allow around two hours to cover the main sights from the Washington Monument to the Lincoln Memorial and around the Tidal Basin. If you get tired of walking, you can hop on the DC Circulator (p196) to see the sights from a city bus. Beware that traffic can be slow moving.

PRACTICAL
INFORMATION

A little local know-how goes a long way in Washington, DC. Here you will find all the essential advice and information you will need during your stay.

AT A GLANCE

EMERGENCY NUMBER

GENERAL
EMERGENCY

911

TIME ZONE

EST/EDT
EDT (Eastern Daylight Time) runs mid-Mar–early Nov
PST -3
GMT +5
JST +13

TAP WATER

Unless otherwise stated, tap water is safe to drink.

WEBSITES AND APPS
DC Eater
Website with the latest restaurant news and food events (*www.dc.eater.com*).

DCist
Local favorite website for city news, events, and openings (*dcist.com*).

DC Metro and Bus
Real-time rail and bus predictions from WMATA (*www.wmata.com*).

Destination DC
DC's comprehensive official tourist information website (*www.washington.org*).

Smithsonian Mobile
A digital guide to the Smithsonian featuring opening hours, floor plans, and special events (*www.si.edu/mobile*).

Personal Security

Washington, DC is generally safe in the tourist areas and most visits are trouble-free. As in many large cities, petty crime does exist, so be alert to your surroundings. Be wary of pickpockets on public transportation and in crowded tourist areas.

If you have anything stolen, report the crime within 24 hours to the nearest police station and take ID with you. If you need to make an insurance claim, get a copy of the crime report.

Contact your embassy if you have your passport stolen, or in the event of a serious crime or accident.

As a rule, Washingtonians are very accepting of all people regardless of their race, gender, or sexuality. DC is a diverse, multicultural city, with a significant African American heritage, one of the largest LGBTQ+ populations in the US, and a strong history of minority activism. Same-sex marriages were legalized in 2009, and in 2013 the district recognized the rights of those wanting to legally change their gender. Destination DC, the city's tourist website (*see side panel*), lists LGBTQ+ events and festivals, bars, and clubs.

Health

The US has a private health care system, and though excellent, it is very expensive. It is therefore very important to arrange comprehensive medical insurance before traveling. The cost of basic care can rise incredibly quickly. You will be asked to pay in advance. Keep all medical receipts for reimbursement later.

Pharmacies are an excellent source of advice. They can diagnose minor ailments and suggest appropriate treatment. Some pharmacies have walk-in clinics attached to treat common illnesses and minor injuries. One such clinic is the **CVS Minute Clinic**, which has nine locations in DC. For immediate treatment in an emergency, call 911 for an ambulance.
CVS Minute Clinic
w cvs.com/minuteclinic

Smoking, Alcohol, and Drugs

Smoking is prohibited in all enclosed public spaces. Cigarettes can be purchased by those over 18 years old; proof of age is required.

The legal minimum age for drinking alcohol in Washington is 21, and you will need photo ID as proof of age. It is illegal to drink alcohol in public parks or to carry an open container of alcohol in your car, and penalties for driving under the influence of alcohol are severe (p197).

Possession of illegal drugs is prohibited and could result in a prison sentence.

ID

It is not compulsory to carry ID at all times in Washington, DC. If you are asked by police to show your ID, a photocopy of your passport (and visa if applicable) should suffice.

Local Customs

Be respectful when visiting national monuments and sights of national significance.

You can be fined for littering. Dispose of your waste in garbage cans. Use the blue bins on the National Mall and in most museums to recycle bottles and cans.

Visiting Churches and Cathedrals

Out of respect, ensure that you are dressed modestly when visiting religious buildings; cover your torso and upper arms; ensure shorts and skirts cover your knees.

Cell Phones and Wi-Fi

Free Wi-Fi hotspots can be found throughout Washington, DC, in public libraries, parks, and throughout the Golden Triangle area. Visit the **Washington DC Free Wi-Fi Access** website to find the nearest free Wi-Fi spot near you. Free Wi-Fi is also available in all underground Metrorail stations. Cafés and restaurants will usually permit the use of their Wi-Fi on the condition that you make a purchase and some hotels offer free Wi-Fi to guests.

Cell phone service in Washington is excellent. If you are coming from overseas and want to guarantee that your cell phone will work, make sure you have a quad-band phone. Check with your service provider before you travel; you may also need to activate the "roaming" facility. Other options include buying a prepaid cell phone in the US or a SIM chip for a US carrier.
Washington DC Free Wi-Fi Access
w octo.dc.gov/wifi

Mail

US Postal Service (**USPS**) runs the postal system in the US. Stamps can be purchased from most major supermarkets and in post offices – most are open from 9am to 5pm Monday to Friday, with a limited Saturday service, usually 9am to noon.

Blue mailboxes are for letters only. Small packages must be taken to a post office. Depending on how far the mail needs to travel in the US, it can take from one to five days to arrive at its destination.
USPS
w usps.com

Taxes and Refunds

Taxes will be added to hotel and restaurant charges, theater tickets, some grocery and store sales, and most other purchases. Always check if tax is included in the price displayed. Sales tax is 6 percent, hotel tax is 14.95 percent, and there is a 10 percent tax on food and beverages.

When tipping in a restaurant, it is the norm to include the tax in your calculation. A quick way to calculate restaurant tips is simply to double the tax, which adds up to about 18 percent.

Discount Cards

Washington, DC offers a number of visitor passes and discount cards (available to buy online and from participating tourist offices) for exhibitions, events, museum entry, and even transportation. These include the **Go Washington DC Pass** and the **Washington DC Sightseeing Pass**. Entry to all Smithsonian sites is free.
Go Washington DC Pass
w gocity.com/washington-dc/en-us
Washington DC Sightseeing Pass
w sightseeingpass.com/en/washington-dc

INDEX

Page numbers in **bold** refer to main entries

9/11 44, 170
14th and U Streets, NW **152**

ACKNOWLEDGMENTS

DK would like to thank the following for their contribution to the previous edition: Susan Burke, Paul Franklin, Taraneh Jerven, Helen Peters, Alice Powers, Jennifer Quasha, Kem Sawyer.

The publisher would like to thank the following for their kind permission to reproduce their photographs:

Key: a-above; b-below/bottom; c-center; f-far; l-left; r-right; t-top

123RF.com: Jon Bilous 168-9; James Kirkikis 178cr; Visions Of America LLC 154br; Gary Tognoni 173b.

500px: John Jack Photography 6-7, Michael Shake 16cl, 50-1.

Alamy Stock Photo: AA World Travel Library 57tr; age fotostock 126bl; Bill Bachmann 189tr; Peter Barritt 33c; Jon Bilous 34-5b; Pat & Chuck Blackley 183clb; Hunter Bliss 11br; Kristina Blokhin 10clb; Joerg Boethling 8cl; B Christopher 151t; David Coleman 86bl, 137clb; Everett Collection Inc 42crb, / Ron Harvey 44crb; Rob Crandall 22t, 31cla, 162-3t, / Alexander Calder © 2018 Calder Foundation, New York/DACS London 2018 Cheval Rouge (1974) 20bl / Simon Crumpton 19bl, 174-5; Ian Dagnall 38tl, 123tl, 131br; Beth Dixson 16cb, 62-3; Randy Duchaine 92cra; Everett Collection Historical 29tr, 55bc; Paul Fearn 114t, 114cra; Michael Flippo 97cl; Glasshouse Images / Circa Images 46bl Jeffrey Isaac Greenberg 2 32bl; Granger Historical Picture Archive 55bl; Nick Higham 156bl; Ian Dagnall Commercial Collection 126cl; imageBROKER 72-3t, 165cr; Archive Images 43tl; JeffG 146-7; LOOK Die Bildagentur der Fotografen GmbI 26-7b; MediaPunch Inc 111clb; Andrei Medvedev 128b; Dominick Miserandino 42br; Mira 29crb, 48–49; W. G. Murray 100tr, 127tl; National Geographic Creative 129t; Newscom 142-3t; NG Images 40bl; North Wind Picture Archives 109tl; NPS Photo 183bl; Michele Oenbrink 22bl; Efrain Padro 80-1b; parkerphotography 36-37t; Painting / Lyman Sayen, The Thundershower. Circa 1917-1918. Tempera on wood. Smithsonian American Art Museum, Washington 94bl; Sean Pavone 12tl, 98b, 144-5t; Chuck Pefley 139bl; Science History Images / Photo Researchers 45bl; Pictorial Press Ltd 141tc; Herb Quick 12-3b; M Ramírez / Robert Berks Studio Inc- All rights reserved Albert Einstein Centennial Monument (1979) 34tr; Edwin Remsberg 13br; Cheryl Rinzler 58tl, 124b, 137bl; RosalreneBetancourt 10 187tl; The Reading Room 43cb, UPI / Richard Ellis 47cra; Philip Scalia 13t, 150bl; Kumar Sriskandan 96br; Stockimo / SJ Cerutti 161cla; Mark Summerfield 22cr, 25tr, 154tl, 185cra, Sueddeutsche Zeitung Photo / Scherl 45cb; Dennis Tarnay, Jr. 171tl; The Protected Art Archive 153bc; Gary Tognoni 27crb; Travelwide / Robert Berks Studio Inc. -All Rights Reserved John F. Kennedy bust (1971) 33br; Tribune Content Agency LLC 81tc; Steve Tulley / Monitor Korean War Veterans Memorial Foundation Inc. Memorial Design - Korean War Veterans Memorial Advisory Board, Architects- Cooper and Lecky Architects; Inc., Sculptor - Frank Gaylord, Muralist - Louis Nelson 84t; Valentin Valkov 141ftr; Michael Ventura 96-7t, 123cr; Vespasian 144bc; Ivan Vdovin 170-71b; WENN Ltd / © Niki de Saint Phalle Charitable Art Foundation / ADAGP, Paris and DACS, London 2018 One of Three Graces Statues (1999) 99tc; World History Archive 141tl; Jennifer Wright 70bl; ZUMA Press, Inc. / Jay Mallin 24-25b, 35cl.

Arena Stage at the Mead Center for American Theater: Bing Thom Architects / Nic Lehoux 18bl, 132-3.

C&O Canal National Historical Park: Roy Roberts 122cr.

Depositphotos Inc: mannaggia 42t.

Dreamstime.com: Alexandersr 55crb; Jon Bilous 8cla, 17br, 26-7t, 31crb, 87br, 104-5, 122-3b, 123tr, 165tl, 166t, 182-3t; Gary Blakeley 61tl; Hunter Bliss 30-1t; Bratty1206 17tl, 88-9; Orhan cam 61br; Chiyacat / Robert Indiana © Morgan Art Foundation Ltd. / Artists Rights Society (ARS), New York, DACS, London 2018 AMOR (2006) 41cl; Giuseppe Crimeni 139br; Cvandyke 27cla, 172tc; Dinhhang 40cl; F11photo 75cra, 75crb; Flashbacknyc 183crb; Frank Fell 160-61b;

Richard Gunion 136-7t; Jasmina 93tl; Kmiragaya 74, 139cra; Massimo Lama 161crb; Erik Lattwein 22crb; Littleny 157tr; Ltisha 143b; Lunamarina 130bl; Jill Meyer 47bl; Nickjene 117cr; Oleschwander 79fcrb; OnAir2 109ftr; Sean Pavone 184b; William Perry 112tc; ZHI QI 38-9b; Abel Roman 47crb; Sborisov 108-9b; Siempreverde22 161c; Daniel Thornberg 186-7b; Inna Zakharchenko 47tr; Zrfphoto 28bl.

Dumbarton Oaks Research Library And Collections, Washington, D.C.: 125t.

Farmers Restaurant Group: Ken Flecther 40cla.

Getty Images: AFP 45cra; AFP/ Karen Bleier 75bl, / Eva Hambach 39tr, 165tr, / Saul Loeb 37bt, 41tr, 41bl,111crb, / Jewel Samad 37cla, / Paul J. Richards 35t, 41cl; Doug Armand 10-1b; Bettmann 43tr, 44tl, 101tr, Sisse Brimberg 2-3; Buyenlarge 155br; CQ-Roll Call Group / Bill Clark 13cr, / Tom Williams 40cr; Elan Fleisher / LOOK-foto 138; Kenneth Garrett 123br; Jon Hicks 103tl; Hulton Archive 80tr, / Alex Wong 110br; Archive Photos / MPI 43cla; Julie Thurston Photography 30-1b; Tasos Katopodis 112b; The LIFE Picture Collection / Francis Miller 46tl; MikeBagley64 185tr; Mooney Photography / Kelly 38tl, 118-9; Richard T. Nowitz 82-3t; Photolibrary / Barry Winiker 108cra; Publisher Mix / © Felix De Weldon Iwo Jima Memorial (1995) / Gavin Hellier 19tr,158; Caroline Purser 190-1b; Astrid Riecken 41br; George Rinhart 109tc; SuperStock 44bl; Universal History Archive 29cla, 44–45t, 45tr; Visions Of Our Land 54bl; VisionsofAmerica / Joe Sohm 55fbr; The Washington Post 12bl, 24tl, 25clb, 25br, 36br, 46-47t, 101b, 137cr, 152t, / Jahi Chikwendiu 41tl, / Katherine Frey 40cra, / Marvin Joseph 40br, / Nikki Kahn 41cr, / Matt McClain 113tr, / Josh Sisk 20crb; Barry Winiker 111bl.

Courtesy of the International Spy Museum: Mark Finkenstaedt 141b; Sam Kittner 140clb, 140bc; Dominique Muñoz 140-1b.

iStockphoto.com: davidevison 11cr; dkfielding 4; Thomas Faull 178-79b; kickstand 46crb; miralex 97crb; Sean Pavone 8-9b, 56-7b; RiverNorthPhotography 103br; RomanBabakin 10cl.

Library of Congress, Washington, DC: LC-DIG-pga-02159 43bl

Courtesy of National Park Service: Abbie Row 109tr.

National Air and Space Museum, Smithsonian Institution: 8clb, 70-1b, 71tl, 71tr, 73bl; Eric F Long 71ftr; Eric Long 20t, 71tc, 72bl, 73tr, 181crb; Dane Penland 73clb, 180, 181clb, 181bl; Carolyn Russo 73crb.

National Gallery Of Art: 21cr, 66-7b, 67cla; Mark Rothko © 1998 Kate Rothko Prizel & Christopher Rothko ARS, NY and DACS, London 2018 Works by Rothko in the, National Gallery's modern art collections 68t; Alexander Calder © 2018 Calder Foundation, New York/DACS London 2018 Untitled, (1976) 68-9b; Ailsa Mellon Bruce Fund 67tl; Collection of Mr. and Mrs. Paul Mellon 1983.1.24 69clb; Corcoran Collection (Museum Purchase, William A. Clark Fund) 67tr; Samuel H. Kress Collection 1952.2.2 69tr.

National Museum of African American History and Culture: 79clb, 79cb, 79crb; Alan Karchmer 28-9t, 78clb, 78crb, 78bl, 79t.

National Portrait Gallery, Smithsonian Institution: 93cr, 95bl.

Rex by Shutterstock: EPA-EFE / Shawn Thew / Amy Sherald First Lady Michelle Obama (2018) – National Portrait Gallery, Smithsonian Institution; gift of Kate Capshaw and Steven, Spielberg; Judith Kern and Kent Whealy; Tommie L. Pegues and Donald A., Capoccia; Clarence, DeLoise, and Brenda Gaines; Jonathan and Nancy Lee Kemper; The Stoneridge Fund of Amy and Marc Meadows; Robert E. Meyerhoff and Rheda, Becker; Catherine and Michael Podell; Mark and Cindy Aron; Lyndon J. Barrois and, Janine Sherman Barrois; The Honorable John and Louise Bryson; Paul and Rose, Carter; Bob and Jane Clark; Lisa R. Davis; Shirley Ross Davis and Family; Alan and, Lois Fern; Conrad and Constance Hipkins;

Sharon and John Hoffman; Audrey M., Irmas; John Legend and Chrissy Teigen; Eileen Harris Norton; Helen Hilton Raiser; Philip and Elizabeth Ryan; Roselyne Chroman Swig; Josef Vascovitz and Lisa, Goodman; Eileen Baird; Dennis and Joyce Black Family Charitable Foundation; Shelley Brazier; Aryn Drake-Lee; Andy and Teri Goodman; Randi Charno Levine and, Jeffrey E. Levine; Fred M. Levin and Nancy Livingston, The Shenson Foundation; Monique Meloche Gallery, Chicago; Arthur Lewis and Hau Nguyen; Sara and John, Schram; Alyssa Taubman and Robert Rothman 95tr.

Shutterstock: littlenySTOCK 161tr

Smithsonian American Art Museum: Mary Cassatt, The Caress, 1902, oil on canvas, Smithsonian American Art Museum, Gift of William T. Evans, 1911.2.1 94cr; Ken Rahaim 92-3b, 94t; Nam June Paik @ Nam June Paik Estate Electronic Superhighway: Continental U.S., Alaska, Hawaii (1995) fifty-one channel video installation (including one closed-circuit, television feed), custom electronics, neon lighting, steel and wood; color, sound Gift of the artist 32-3tc.

Courtesy of the Smithsonian's National Museum of American History: 76cl, 76-7b, 77tl, 77tr, 77cla.

Courtesy of Leo Villareal: James Ewing / Leo Villareal Multiverse (2008) -LEDs, custom softftware & electrical hardware, suspension material Site-specific permanent installations, National Gallery of the Arts Washington, DC 11tr.

Front flap images:
Alamy Stock Photo: Hunter Bliss cla; Rob Crandall bl; Ian Dagnall t; Herb Quick cra; **Getty Images:** Doug Armand br; **iStockphoto.com:** Sean Pavone c.

Sheet map cover images:
iStockphoto.com: Sean Pavone

Cover images:
Front and spine: **iStockphoto.com:** Sean Pavone.
Back: **Alamy Stock Photo:** Philip Scalia c; **Dreamstime. com:** Jon Bilous tr; **Getty Images:** Eric Sturdivant cla; **iStockphoto.com:** Sean Pavone b.

For further information see: www.dkimages.com

Illustrators:
Stephen Conlin, Gary Cross, Richard Draper, Chris Orr & Associates, Mel Pickering, Robbie Polley, John Woodcock

Penguin Random House

This edition updated by
Contributor Stephen Keeling
Senior Editor Alison McGill
Senior Designers Tania Da Silva Gomes, Stuti Tiwari
Project Editors Parnika Bagla, Rada Radojicic
Project Art Editor Ankita Sharma
Assistant Editor Mark Silas
Picture Research Manager Taiyaba Khatoon
Assistant Picture Research Administrator Vagisha Pushp
Jacket Coordinator Bella Talbot
Jacket Designer Jordan Lambley
Senior Cartographers Subhashree Bharati, Mohammad Hassan
Cartography Manager Suresh Kumar
DTP Designer Tanveer Zaidi
Senior Production Editor Jason Little
Production Controller Kariss Ainsworth
Deputy Managing Editor Beverly Smart
Managing Editors Shikha Kulkarni, Hollie Teague
Managing Art Editor Bess Daly
Senior Managing Art Editor Priyanka Thakur
Art Director Maxine Pedliham
Publishing Director Georgina Dee

First edition 2000

Published in Great Britain by Dorling Kindersley Limited, DK, One Embassy Gardens, 8 Viaduct Gardens, London SW11 7BW

The authorised representative in the EEA is Dorling Kindersley Verlag GmbH. Arnulfstr. 124, 80636 Munich, Germany

Published in the United States by DK Publishing, 1450 Broadway, Suite 801, New York, NY 10018

Copyright © 2000, 2022 Dorling Kindersley Limited
A Penguin Random House Company
21 22 23 24 10 9 8 7 6 5 4 3 2 1

A CIP catalog record for this book is available from the British Library.

A catalog record for this book is available from the Library of Congress.

ISSN: 1542 1554
ISBN: 978 0 2415 5937 6

Printed and bound in China.

www.dk.com

A NOTE FROM DK EYEWITNESS

The rapid rate at which the world is changing is constantly keeping the DK Eyewitness team on our toes. While we've worked hard to ensure that this edition of Washington, DC is accurate and up-to-date, we know that opening hours alter, standards shift, prices fluctuate, places close and new ones pop up in their stead. So, if you notice we've got something wrong or left something out, we want to hear about it. Please get in touch at travelguides@dk.com